Jesus is Calling You!
You may have a calling on your life!

Hazelteen Wilson

Jesus is Calling You!
You may have a calling on your life!
Copyright © 2023 by Hazelteen Wilson

All rights reserved. No part of this publication may be reproduced, distributed, or transmitted in any form or by any means, including photocopying, recording, or other electronic or mechanical methods, without the prior written permission of the publisher or author, except in the case of brief quotations embodied in critical reviews and certain other noncommercial uses permitted by copyright law.

Although every precaution has been taken to verify the accuracy of the information contained herein, the author and publisher assume no responsibility for any errors or omissions. No liability is assumed for damages that may result from the use of information contained within.

Library of Congress Control Number: 2022919475
ISBN-13:   Paperback: 978-1-64749-854-2
          ePub: 978-1-64749-855-9

Printed in the United States of America

GoToPublish LLC
1-888-337-1724
www.gotopublish.com
info@gotopublish.com

Jesus Is Calling You

Jesus Christ was born human after existing in Heaven because He wanted us to know the true meaning of God. He wanted us to know what He has for us on this earth to accomplish, and to learn His purpose, and will for our lives.

In Jesus Is Calling You, we will look at Jesus Christ's teachings and his purpose for our lives while we are here on earth. We will look at some passages that will cover these topics inside this Bible Study, mostly pertaining to John and a few other scriptures as well.

Place and Date of Writing, Audience, Occasion and Purpose:

The date of the writing was close to the destruction of the temple in Jerusalem. The reason for the writing was to reach diaspora Jews and Gentiles attracted to Judaism (Proselytes). It was written around AD 70 but not immediately after the destruction of Jerusalem (Kostenberger 25).

In this chapter, we have an account of the birth and infancy of our Lord Jesus having had notice of his conception, and of the birth and infancy of his forerunner, in the former chapter. The first-begotten is here brought into the world; let us go meet Him with our hosannas, blessed is He that cometh. Here is, I (http://www.biblestudytools.com).

In the book of John, there are teachings of Jesus Christ that informs us on how He wants us to work until the day that He comes for us. We are going to look at some of these Scriptures, answer some questions, and make observations and insights about what we find. As Christians, our main focus should be what God has put us on this earth to accomplish His will for our lives and why should we work toward this calling?

Are we His disciples and do we love God and one another? Jesus wants us to minister to others about His gift of salvation. Do we fit for the master's hand?

We can find out these things by taking a close look at His **Incarnation**, what His **Incarnation** is, and did it happen, was He born fully God and fully man? We will look at Jesus Christ's **Miracles,** and what was the importance of the **Miracles?**

We will search for the truth of the scriptures and see if what we learn from the Bible is true.

Internal Evidence

"The Word became flesh and made his dwelling among us. We have seen his glory, the glory of the One and Only, who came from the Father, full of grace and truth" (John 1:14). This is the opening testimony of John's Gospel. Who are the "we" who have seen Jesus' glory? When Jesus turned water into wine, is that the first miraculous sign? Did Jesus performing at Cana in Galilee revealing His glory?

This is a three-week study, and we will color code what we find and bold it with an ink pen by underlining words. We will study the Scriptures to see if it has clarity and purpose for our lives? Let's get ready to dive in and study the word of God.

As we study Luke, we are going to color the city, town, and country orange, and names of parents red. Color shepherds/angel purple and children brown. We will color God/Lord green in questions 1–8. As we start our study on John, we will use crayons to color the Word pink, and God or He/Him blue, and born or birth yellow from question 9–15. We will count the number of times we see each word in those passages.

Color Jesus' miracles red, color Jesus/His in tan. Color the word "saw" orange, and "God" blue. Colorhe "Rabbi" in purple. Count the number of times they appear.

Luke 2:1–22

(1)In those days. Caesar Augustus issued a decree that a census should be taken of the entire Roman world. (2) This was the first census that took place while Quirinius was the governor of Syria. (3) And everyone went to their own town to register. (4) So, Joseph also went up from the town of Nazareth in Galilee to Judea, to Bethlehem the town of David, because he belonged to the house and line of David. (5) He went there to register with Mary, who was expecting a child. (6) While they were there, the time came for the baby to be born. (7) And she wrapped him in clothes and placed him in a manger, because there was no guest room available for them. (8) And there were shepherds living out in the fields nearby, keeping watch over their flocks at night. (9) An angel of the Lord appeared to them, and the glory of the Lord shone around them, and they were terrified. (10) But the angel said to them, "Do not be afraid. I bring you good news that will cause great joy for all the people." (11) "Today, in the town of David, a Savior has been born to you; he is the Messiah, the Lord." (12) "This will be a sign to you: You will find a baby wrapped in cloth and lying in a manger." (13) Suddenly, a great company of the heavenly host appeared with the angel, praising God and saying. (14) "Glory to God in the highest heaven, and on the earth peace to those on whom His favor rests." (15) When the angels had left them and gone into heaven, the shepherds said to one another. "Let's go to Bethlehem and see this thing that has happened, which the Lord has told us about." (16) So, they hurried off and found Mary and Joseph, and the baby, who was lying in the manger. (17) When they had seen him, they spread the word about what had been told to them about this child. (18) And all who heard it were amazed at what the shepherds said to them. (19) But Mary treasured all these things and pondered them in her heart. (20) The shepherds returned, glorifying and praising God for all the things they had been told. (21) On the eighth, when it was time to circumcise the child, he was named Jesus, the name the angel had given him before he was conceived. (22) When the time came for the purification rites required by the Law of Moses, Joseph and Mary took him to Jerusalem to present him to the Lord." (Holman 1043-44).

What observations were made:

What insights were made:

What applications will you make:

Week 1: We will look at the Incarnation and Miracles. Read the verses below.

1.   Was Jesus really born here on earth?

2.   Who were His parents?

3.   Where was Jesus born?

4.   What description did you read about His birth?

5.   How was Jesus conceived?

In the beginning

"In the beginning" a timeless beginning. Thus, we could translate the first part of the verse as "in eternity the Word existed. The Greek term is *logos*. In the Hebrew language of the Old Testament, "The Word is described as an agent of creation (Psalm 33:6). The source of God's message to His people is through the prophets (Hosea 1:2) and "God's law, His standard of holiness" (Psalm 119:11, Life Application Bible Commentary 2–3).

Now, we are going to go farther in the lesson to give deeper meaning to what was just studied. We will begin week two looking at Jesus Christ's **Preexistence**. Did Jesus exist before coming to earth? How does His **Preexistence** help us to understand who Jesus Christ is? Next, we will look at the **Resurrection** and its significance in our lives. What does this mean for us as believers of Christ? What hope should we cling on to as believers? How does week one work play a part of week two?

In John 1: 1–14, he talks about Jesus' pre-existence and the creation itself. As John tells the story, he explains the incarnation of the Word. How is Jesus Christ incarnated? What takes place to let us know that He existed before the creation of the world? Who is there when creation takes place?

The verse describes the status of Christ as He existed before the creation of the world—that is, His preincarnate state. The words in Greek are a present participle indicating continuing existence from the beginning (Genesis 1:1). Jesus Christ was not merely a human who lived for thirty-three years on this earth; instead, He existed with God before time began. In Jesus' prayer before His death, He said, "And now, Father, glorify me in Your presence with the glory I had with You before the world began." (John 17:5 Life Application Bible Commentary 57).

The Resurrection

John's account of Jesus' crucifixion is somber and restrained. Jesus carried his own cross. He went to the Place of the Skull (called Golgotha in Aramaic; the Latin term is Calvary). He was crucified with two others, one on his left and the other on his right (Life Application Bible Commentary 181).

Chapter 20 opens on the third day after Jesus' crucifixion and burial, early "on the first day of the week (Sunday)." Mary Magdalene, one of Jesus' most committed female followers (19:25), went to the tomb when it was still dark and found that the stone had been removed from the entrance (Life Application Bible Commentary 182).

As we start our study on John, we will use crayons to color the WORD pink, and "God" or "He/Him" blue, also the word "born or birth" yellow from questions 1–8. We count the number of times we see each word in those passages. For questions 9–15, we will color names orange. Color "God/Father/Jesus/Holy Spirit" tan. The word "disciples" gray. Color names red. Color Jewish leaders purple. Color the word "see/saw" and then underline it.

John 1: 1--4

(1) In the beginning was the Word, and the Word was God. (2) He was with God in the beginning. (3) Through Him, all things were made; without Him, nothing was made that has been made. (4) In Him was life, and that life was the light of all mankind. (5) The light shines in the darkness, and the darkness has not overcome it. (6) There was a man sent from God whose name was John. (7) He came as a witness to testify about that light, so that through Him, all might believe. (8) He himself was not the light; he came only as a witness to the light. (9) The true light that gives light to everyone was coming into the world. (10) He was in the world, and though the world was made through Him, the world did not recognize him. (11) He came to that which was His own, but His own did not receive Him. (12) Yet to all who did receive him, to those who believed in His name, He gave the right to become children of God. (13) Children born not of natural descent, nor of human decision, or a husband's will, but born of God. (14) The Word became flesh, and made His dwelling among us. We have seen His glory, the glory of the one and only Son, who came from the Father, full of grace and truth.

Week 2: We will take a glance at the ***Preexistence.*** Read the verses below:

1. What is taking place in these passages?
   John 1:1–5

2. How was Jesus before creation?
   John 1:2–3

3. How was John a witness?
   John 1:6–7

4. How was the world made, and who did it not recognize?
   John 1:8–11

5. Why did Jesus have the right to have us become children of God?
   John 1:12–13

6. How were these Children of God born?
   John 1:13

7. What did the word do?
   John 1:14

8. Who did the word dwell around and how have we seen the word glory?
   John 1:14

9. What did Mary Magdalene see when she went to the tomb?
   John 20:1–2

10. How many Disciples of Jesus Christ were there at the site?
    John 20:3–4

11. Who went to the tomb and what did they find?
    John 20:5-7

12. When the other disciples reached the tomb what happened?
    John 20:8–9

13. How did Mary respond when she saw Jesus Christ?
    John 20:13–15

14. How was Jesus going to ascend into heaven?
    John 20:16–17

15. What did Mary do after experiencing all that happened?
    John 20:18

What ***Observations*** did you make in this study of ***Preexistence*** (questions 1–8) and ***Resurrection*** (questions 9–15)? What ***insights*** did you see and what did the scriptures reflect about your life?

Luke 2:25–33

25.) Now there was a man in Jerusalem called Simeon, who was righteous and devout. He was waiting for the consolation of Israel, and the Holy Spirit was on him. 26.) It had been revealed to him by the Spirit, and he went into the temple courts. When the parents brought in the child Jesus to do for him what the custom of the Law required. 28.) Simeon took him in his arms and praised God, saying: 29.) "Sovereign Lord, as you have promised, you may now dismiss your servant in peace. 30.) For my eyes have seen your servant in peace. 30.) For my eyes have seen your salvation. 31.) Which you have prepared in the sight of all nations: 32.) A light for revelation to the Gentiles, and the glory of your people Israel. 33.) The child's father and mother marveled at what was said about him (Holman 1044)."

What Observations have you made:

What Insights have you made:

What applications have you made:

Week 3

1. Who was Simon?

2. What was Simon waiting on?

3. What was revealed to him?

4. What was required by law for Simon to do? Why?

5. Why did Simon take the child Jesus into his arms?

6. How did Simon see the salvation of the Lord?

7.   How was this a light to the Gentiles?

8.   What did the child Jesus' parents do?

9.   What was this child destined to cause?

10. How will the child Jesus be spoken against?

11. How will hearts be revealed?

12. How will a sword pierce our own hearts?

Matthew Henry's Concise Commentary on Luke 2:25–35

The same Spirit that provided for the support of Simon's hope, provided for his joy. Those who would see Christ must go to his temple. Here is a confession of his faith, that this Child in his arms was the Savior, the salvation itself, the salvation of God's appointing. He bids farewell to this world. How poor does this world look to one that has Christ in his arms, and salvation in his view! See here, how comfortable is the death of a good man; he departs in peace with God, peace with his own conscience, in peace with death. Those that have welcomed Christ, may welcome death. Joseph and Mary marveled at the things which were spoken of this Child. Simon shows them likewise, what reason they had to rejoice with trembling. And Jesus, his doctrine, and people, are still spoken against; his truth and holiness are still denied and blasphemed; his preached word is still the touchstone of men's characters. The secret good affections in the minds of some will be revealed by their embracing Christ; the secret corruptions of others will be revealed by their enmity to Christ. Men will be judged by the thoughts of their hearts concerning Christ. He shall be a suffering Jesus; his mother shall suffer with him, because of the nearness of her relation and affection (Henry 1).

Luke 2:36–40

36.) There was also a prophet, Anna, the daughter of Penuel, of the tribe of Asher. She was very old; she had lived with her husband seven years after her marriage, 37.) And then was a widow until she was eighty-four. She never left the temple but worshiped night and day, fasting and praying. 38.) Coming up to them at that very moment, she gave thanks to God and spoke about the child to all who were looking forward to the redemption of Jerusalem. 39.) When Joseph and Mary had done everything required by the Law of the Lord, they returned to Galilee, to their own town of Nazareth. 40.) And the child grew and became strong; he was filled with wisdom, and the grace of God was on Him (Holman 1044)."

What Observations have you made:

What Insights have you made:

What Applications have you made:

Week 4:

1.   Who is Anna?

2.   How long did she live with her husband?

3.   How did she worship God?

4. How did the child represent redemption?

5. How did Mary and Joseph do what was required by law?

6. What was the child Jesus filled with?

7. Why was the grace of God on this child Jesus?

Matthew Henry's Concise Commentary on Luke 2:36-40

There was much evil then in the church, yet God left not Himself without witness. Anna always dwelt in, or at least attended at, the temple. She was always in a praying spirit; gave herself to prayer, and in all things, she served God. Those to whom Christ is made known, have great reason to thank the Lord. She taught others about Him. Let the example of the venerable saints, Simon and Anna, give courage to those whose hairy heads are, like theirs, a crown of glory, being found in the way of righteousness. The lips soon to be silent in the grave, should be showing forth the praises of the Redeemer. In all things, it became Christ to be made like unto His brethren. Therefore, he passed through infancy and childhood as other children; yet without sin, and with manifest proofs of the Divine nature in Him. By the Spirit of God, all his faculties performed their offices in a manner not seen in anyone else. Other children have foolishness bound in their hearts, which appears in what they say or do, but He was filled with wisdom, by the influence of the Holy Ghost. Everything He said and did, was wisely said and wisely done, above His years. Other children show the corruption of their nature; nothing but the grace of God was upon Him (Henry 1)."

Luke 2: 41–51

41.) Every year, Jesus' parents went to Jerusalem for the Festival of the Passover. 42.) When He was twelve years old, they went up to the festival, according to the custom. 43.) After the festival was over, while His parents were returning home, the boy Jesus stayed behind in Jerusalem, but they were unaware of it. 44.) Thinking He was in their company, they traveled on for a day. Then they began looking for Him among their relatives and friends. 45.) When they did not find Him, they went back to Jerusalem to look for Him. 46.) After three days, they found Him in the temple courts, sitting among the teachers, listening to them and asking them questions. 47.) Everyone who heard Him was amazed at His understanding and His answers. 48.) When His parents saw Him, they were astonished. His mother said to Him, "Son, why have you treated us like this? Your father and I have been anxiously searching for you." 49.) "Why were you searching for me?" He asked. "Didn't you know I had to be in my Father's house?" 50.) But they did not understand what He was saying to them.

51.) Then He went down to Nazareth with them and was obedient to them. But His mother treasured all these things in her heart. 52.) And Jesus grew in wisdom and stature, and in favor with God and man.

What Observations have you made:

What Insights have you made:

What Applications have you made:

Week 5:

1. How did Jesus and his parents celebrate the passover?

2. Why would the child Jesus stay behind after the passover?

3. Why were Jesus' parents looking for him?

4. What was the child Jesus doing when His parents found Him?

5. How did the child Jesus respond to His parents?

6. Why would the child Jesus say that He was in His Father's house?

7. Why do you think His parents did not understand Him?

8. Why was He obedient to His parents?

9. How did His mother show her feelings for what He was doing?

10. Why is this the second time the Bible states he grew in wisdom and stature?

Life Application Bible Commentary on John 1:1–18

Jesus revealed His essential nature in what He taught and did. John wrote about Jesus as fully human and fully God." Although Jesus took upon Himself full humanity and entered history with the limitations of a human being, He never ceased to be the eternal God, eternally existing, the Creator and Sustainer of all things, and the source of eternal life. John's gospel tells the truth about Jesus, the foundation of all truth. If we cannot or do not believe in Jesus' true identity, we will not be able to trust our eternal destiny to Him (Tyndale 1). John wrote his Gospel to build our faith and confidence in Jesus Christ so that we might believe that Jesus truly was and is the Son of God (John 20:30–31).

John starts at the "beginning," with the first eighteen verses of John, called the prologue. Many commentators consider the prologue to be a poem or, at least, rhythmical prose. Some commentators suggest that verses 1–5, 10–12, and 14–18 may have been parts of one or several early Christian hymns. Others have thought that verses 14–18 were used as an early church confessional statement, to which John added his stamp of approval (Tyndale 1).

Furthermore, the prologue to John's Gospel provides a miniature of the entire Gospel. John's goal and guiding purpose in writing can be found in almost every phrase of his work. The prolog highlights most of the insights and truths that we find in the rest of the Gospel. John introduced key terms: *the Word, God, life, light, darkness, witness, the world, rejection/reception, belief, regeneration,* (becoming a child of God), *incarnation* (the Word became flesh), *the one and only Son of the Father, glory, grace, truth, fullness.* In the rest of the Gospel, John expanded and illustrated each of these from Jesus' life and ministry (Tyndale1).

John 1:1–14

1.) In the beginning was the Word, and the Word was with God, and the Word was God. 2.) He was with God in the beginning. 3.) Through

Him, all things were made; without him, nothing was made that has been made. 4.) In Him was life and that life was the light of all mankind. 5.) The light shines in the darkness, and the darkness has not overcome it. 6.) There was a man sent from God whose name was John. 7.) He came as a witness to testify about that light. 8.) He himself was not the light; he came only as a witness to the light. 9.) The true light that gives light to everyone was coming into the world. 10.) He was in the world, and though the world was made through Him, the world did not recognize Him. 11.) He came to that which was His own, but His own did not receive H.im. 12) Yet, to all who received Him, to those who believed in His name, He gave the right to become children of God. 13.) Children born not of natural descent, nor of human decision, or a husband's will, but born of God. 14.) The Word became flesh and made His dwelling among us. We have seen His glory, the glory of the one and only Son, who came from the Father full of grace and truth.

What is your Observation?

What is your Insight?

What is your Application?

Week 6:

1. How is the Word explained?

2. Who was the Word?

3. How were all things made through the Word?

4. What was the man's name and where did he come from?

5. Who was he testifying to?

6. Why was He testifying?

7. Who might believe what?

8. How is the true light described?

9. How were they to become children of God?

10. How were they born?

John internal evidence: Life Application Bible Commentary

Jesus turns water to wine: "Beyond the startling and miraculous transformation of water into wine by Jesus, this incident includes two important statements concerning Christ:

(1) "My time has not yet come," and (2) Jesus "revealed His glory" (Barton, Comfort, Veerman, Wilson, Osborne 30).

First, from Jesus we hear, "My time has not yet come" (2:4). In John's Gospel, Jesus' "time" refers to the time of His glorification when He would receive His true place and position as the Son of God. This glorification would include His death and resurrection. Everything Jesus said and did point toward that "time." Jesus' words emphasized His life purpose. Each of the Gospel's expresses this unique self-awareness of Jesus in a different way (Barton, Comfort, Veerman, Wilson, Osborne 30).

John 2:1–12

1.) On the third day a wedding took place at Cana in Galilee. Jesus' mother was there. 2.) And Jesus and His disciples had also been invited to the wedding. 3.) When the wine was gone, Jesus' mother said to Him, "They have no more wine." 4.) "Woman, why do you involve me?" Jesus replied. "My hour has not yet come." 5.) His mother said to the servants, "Do whatever He tells you." 6.) Nearby, stood six stone water jars, the kind used by the Jews for ceremonial washing, each holding from twenty to thirty gallons. 7.) Jesus said to the servants, "Fill the jars with water"; so, they filled them to the brim. 8.) Then he told them, "Now draw some out and take it to the master of the banquet." (9) They did so, and the master of the banquet tasted the water that had been turned into wine. He did not realize where it had come from, though the servants who had drawn the water knew. Then he called the bridegroom aside. 10.) And said, "Everyone, bring out the choice wine first and then the cheaper wine after the guests have had too much to drink; but ye best till now." 11.) What Jesus did here in Cana of Galilee was the first sign through which He revealed His glory, and His disciples believed in Him. 12.) After this, He went down to Capernaum with His mother and brothers and disciples. There, they stayed for a few days (Holman 1082).

What Observations have you made:

What Insights have you made:

What Applications have you made:

Week 7:

1. What was the reason for the celebration?

2. What did they run out of and what happened?

3. What did Jesus' mother ask him?

4. How did Jesus respond?

5. What kind of miracle did Jesus perform?

6. How did this look for the Master?

7. Was this a blessing?

8. What sign was this of Jesus' miracles?

9. What was the wine made from?

10. How was it made?

11. How was this special?

Life Application Bible Commentary on John 3:1–12

It would be difficult to find any other portion of Scripture as well known as John 3:16 or any other statement of Scripture more applied than "You must be born again" (v.7, NKJV). When Jesus revealed the necessity of the new birth to Nicodemus, He exposed mankind's ultimate hope. These are the descriptions from chapter two, those who approach Jesus with 24.) an inadequate faith (Tyndale 49). Nicodemus (vv. 1–15), the Samaritan woman (4:1–42), and the nobleman from Capernaum (4:43–54) they show who and what Jesus was capable of and meeting Him face to face changed their view and their lives (Tyndale 49).

Wherever Jesus went, changes occurred and He challenged systems, powers, and individuals (Tyndale 49). In chapter three, Nicodemus gets the spotlight as a person who was either a typical example of someone to whom Jesus could not entrust himself (2:24) or he was an exception to the rule—a person to whom Jesus could entrust himself (Tyndale 49). Nicodemus was one of the Pharisees—the strictest, most conservative, and traditional Jewish sect of those times (Tyndale 51). The Jewish religious leaders were divided into several groups Pharisees and Sadducees (Tyndale 51). The Pharisees separated themselves from anything non-Jewish and carefully followed both Old Testament laws and the oral traditions handed down through the centuries (Tyndale 51). The Sadducees, on the other hand, were the elite priestly class who freely mixed their political agenda with the power they wielded as religious leaders (Tyndale 51). Nicodemus was also a member of the Jewish council. The Jewish ruling body was the council (sometimes called the Sanhedrin) made up of seventy-one of Israel's religious leaders. Nicodemus was a very prominent figure in Israel, representing the cream of the nation. In fact, Jesus called him "a teacher of Israel (3:10 NRSV)" (Tyndale 51).

John 3:1–12

1.) Now, there was a Pharisee, a man named Nicodemus who was a member of the Jewish ruling council. 2.) He came to Jesus at night and said, "Rabbi, we know that You are a teacher who has come from God. For no one could perform the signs You are doing if God were not with You." 3.) Jesus replied, "Very truly I tell you, no one can see the kingdom of God unless they are born again." 4.) "How can someone be born when they are old?" Nicodemus asked. "Surely they cannot enter a second time into their mother's womb to be born!" 5.) Jesus answered, "Very truly I tell you, no one can enter the kingdom of God unless they are born of water and the Spirit. 6.) Flesh gives birth to flesh, but the spirit gives birth to spirit. 7.) You should not be surprised at my saying; you must be born again. 8.) The wind blows where it pleases, you hear its sound, but you cannot tell where it comes from or where it is going. So, it is with everyone born of the Spirit." 9.) "How can this be?" Nicodemus asked. 10.) "You are Israel's teacher," said Jesus, "And do you not understand these things? 11.) Very truly I tell you, we speak of what we know, and we testify to what we have seen, but still, you people do not accept our testimony. 12.) I have spoken to you of earthly things, and you do not believe; how then will you believe if I speak of heavenly things? 13.) No one has ever gone into heaven except the one who came from heaven—the Son of Man. 14.) Just as Moses lifted the snake in the wilderness, so the Son of Man must be lifted, 15.) That everyone who believes may have eternal life in him. 16.) For God so loved the world that He gave His one and only Son, that whoever believes in Him shall not perish but have eternal life. 17.) For God did not send His Son into the world to condemn the world, but to save the world through Him. 18.) Whoever believes in Him is not condemned, but whoever does not believe in the name of God's one and only Son. 19.) This is the verdict: Light has come into the world, but people loved darkness instead of light because their deeds were evil. 20.) Everyone who does evil hates the light and will not come into the light for fear that their deeds will be exposed. 21.) But whoever lives by the truth comes into the light, so that it may be seen plainly that what they have done has been done in the sight of God (Holman 1083)."

What are your Observations?

What are your Insights?

What are your Applications?

Week 8:

1.   Who is Nicodemus?

2.   What did Nicodemus say to Jesus?

3.   How did Nicodemus know that God was with Jesus Christ?

4.   How did Jesus answer Nicodemus?

5. How was Jesus' answer important to Nicodemus?

6. Why did Nicodemus ask how can a man be born again?

7. What did Nicodemus not understand?

8. How did Jesus say someone had to be born again?

9. What did Jesus mean when he said, "That which is born of flesh is flesh, and that which is born of the spirit is spirit?"

10. Why did Nicodemus still not understand what Jesus was teaching him?

Life Application Bible Commentary on the Samaritan Woman

Jesus had to pass through Samaria on His way to Galilee. In Jesus encounter with the Samaritan woman and with the Samaritans in Sychar, He revealed that He is "the gift of God" (4:10), who gives "a fountain of water springing up into everlasting life" (4:14 NKJV) to teach believers. He also revealed that He is the "expected Messiah" (4:22–26, Tyndale 75). Furthermore, Jesus pointed the Samaritans to the truth about salvation, God's nature, and the worship of God. Salvation comes from among the Jews (the Messiah is a Jew), God is spirit, and God must be worshiped in spirit and truth.

John 4:1–19

1.) Now Jesus learned that the Pharisees had heard that He was gaining and baptizing more disciples. 2.) So, he left Judea and went back once more to Galilee. 3.) Now he had to go through Samaria. 4.) So, He came to a town in Samaria called Sychar, near the plot of ground Jacob had given to his son Joseph. 5.) Jacob's well was there, and Jesus, tired as He was from the journey, sat down by the well. It was about noon. 6.) When a Samaritan woman came to draw water, Jesus said to her, "Will you give me a drink?" 7.) His disciples had gone into the town to buy food. 8.) The Samaritan woman said to Him, "You are a Jew, and I am a Samaritan woman. How can you ask me for a drink?" (For Jews do not associate with Samaritans.) 9.) Jesus answered her, "If you knew the gift of God and who it is that asks you for a drink, you would have asked Him, and He would have given you living water." 10.) "Sir," the woman said, "You have nothing to draw with and the well is deep. Where can you get this living water?" 11.) "Are you greater than our father Jacob, who gave us the well and drank from it himself, as did also his sons and his livestock?" 12.) Jesus answered, "Everyone who drinks this water will be thirsty again." 13.) "But whoever drinks the water I give them will never thirst. Indeed, the water I give them will become in them a spring of water welling up to eternal life." 14." The woman said to Him, "Sir, give me this water so that I won't get thirsty and have to keep coming here to draw water." 15.) He told her, "Go, call your husband and come back." 16.) "I have no husband," she replied. Jesus said to her, "You are right when you say you have no husband,."17.) "The fact is, you have had five husbands, and the man you now have is not your husband. What you have just said is quite true." 18.) "Sir," the woman said, "I can see that you are a prophet." 19.) "Our ancestors worshiped on this mountain, but you Jews claim that the place where we must worship is in Jerusalem." 20.) "Woman," Jesus replied, "Believe me, a time is coming when you will worship the Father neither on this mountain nor in Jerusalem." 21.) "You Samaritans worship what you do not know, we worship what we do know. For salvation is from the Jews." 22.) "Yet a time is coming and has now come when the true worshipers will worship the Father in the Spirit and in truth. For they are the kind of worshipers the Father seeks." 23.) "God is Spirit, and His worshipers must worship in the Spirit and in truth." 24.) The woman said, "I know that the Messiah (called Christ) is coming. When He comes, He will explain everything to us." 25.) "I, the one speaking to you—I am He (Holman 1084-85)."

What Observations have you made:

What Insights have you made?

What Applications have you made:

Week 9:

1. What did the Pharisees learn about Jesus?

2. Why did Jesus leave to go to Galilee?

3. Why did Jesus sit at the well?

4. Who was with the Samaritan woman when she came to draw water?

5. Why would Jesus ask the Samaritan woman for a drink?

6. How was it against the law for Jesus to associate with a Samaritan woman?

7. How did Jesus explain to her eternal life?

8. Why did Jesus say, anyone that drinks His water would thirst no more?

9. How did Jesus explain to the Samaritan woman the relationship she has with her husbands?

10. How many husbands did Jesus explain to her? And how many husbands did she have?

Discipleship is a big part of Jesus Christ' calling. While He was on earth, He called many to His Ministry to help bring others in so that they may find the love of God and how His mercies endure forever. Jesus has a calling for us as believers to minister to the poor, the sick, the sexually exploited, the disabled, and the diseased. The list goes on and in so many areas He has called discipleship. In week three, we will look at *discipleship* and how is it a calling on our lives.

Life Application Bible Commentary on Jesus Heals a Lame Man by the Pool: John 5:1–18

God gives salvation freely through Jesus Christ ' (Tyndale 99). But to receive salvation, a person must believe . The lame man by the pool at Bethesda had to want to be healed. Then Jesus approached him later to explain to him that he needed to believe and receive spiritual healing as well God makes the offer and God performs the miracle, but we must respond to His offer and accept it. After this was a feast of the Jews, and Jesus went up to Jerusalem. Capernaum, at the northern end of Israel, was lower in altitude than Jerusalem. Because of Jerusalem's location in the mountains, and because of its priority as the city of David, people spoke of going up to Jerusalem. All Jewish males were required to come to Jerusalem to attend the feast: (1) the Feast of Passover and Unleavened Bread, (2) the Feast of the Weeks (also called Pentecost), and (3) the Feast of Tabernacles. Though this feast is not specified, the phrase explains why Jesus was in Jerusalem. John added the expression of the Jews to help Gentile readers. Now in Jerusalem by the Sheep Gate is a pool. This is how most translators render the Greek. A few other translations render it this way: "Now at the Sheep-Pool in Jerusalem there is a place…" (NEB; see also NJB). Readers familiar with Jerusalem would have known that John was referring to Sheep Gate (It is mentioned in Nehemiah 3:1,32; 12:39). Recent excavations show that this site had two pools with five covered colonnades. These were open structures with roofs that allowed some protection from the weather.

Waiting for the movement of the water (Tyndale 100). For an angel went down at a certain time into the pool and stirred up the water; then whoever stepped in first, after the stirring of the water, was made well of whatever disease he had. It is very doubtful this portion was written by John, since it is not found in the earliest manuscripts, and where it does occur in later manuscripts, it is often marked in such a way as to show that it is an addition. The passage was probably inserted later by scribes who felt it necessary to provide an explanation for the gathering of disabled people and the stirring of the water mentioned in verse 7. It is unclear whether an angel actually disturbed the water, or if this was just a local superstition used to explain the natural movement in a pool of water fed by a spring. But somehow, the waters were stirred and seemed to have had curative powers.

John 5:1–15

1.) Sometime later, Jesus went up to Jerusalem for one of the Jewish festivals. 2.) Now there is in Jerusalem near the Sheep Gate a pool, which in Aramaic is called Bethesda and which is surrounded by five covered colonnades. 3.) Here, a great number of disabled people used to lie—the blind, the lame, the paralyzed (Tyndale 100). 5.) One who was there had been an invalid for thirty-eight years. 6.) When Jesus saw him lying there and learned that he had been in this condition for a long time, he asked him, "Do you want to get well?" 7.) "Sir," the invalid replied, "I have no one to help me into the pool when the water is stirred. While I am trying to get in, someone else goes down ahead of me." 8.) Then Jesus said to him, "Get up! Pick up your mat and walk." 9.) At once, the man was cured. He picked up his mat and walked. The day on which this took place was a Sabbath. 10.) And so, the Jewish leaders said to the man who had been healed, "It is the Sabbath, the law forbids you to carry your mat." 11.) But he replied, "The man who made me well said to me, "Pick up your mat and walk."

12.) So they asked him, "Who is this fellow who told you to pick it up and walk?" 13.) The man who was healed had no idea who it was, for Jesus had slipped away into the crowd that was there. 14.) Later, Jesus found him at the temple and said to him, "See, you are well again. Stop sinning or something worse may happen to you." 15.) The man went away and told the Jewish leaders that it was Jesus who had made him well (Holman 1086).

What is your Observation?

What is your Insight?

What is your Application?

Week 10:

1.   Why was Jesus in Jerusalem?

2.   What is Bethesda and its surroundings?

3.   Who was there?

4.   What was wrong with them?

5. How many years has one man been invalid?

6. Why did Jesus ask the man if he wanted to get well?

7. What was his excuse?

8. What did Jesus tell the man to do?

9. What day did this happen?

10. Why was it forbidden?

11. Did the man know who Jesus was?

12. When Jesus found him what did he tell him to stop doing?

Life Application Bible Commentary on Jesus Feeding Five Thousand/6:1–15

John selects a particular place for presenting a spiritual truth about Christ (Tyndale 121). Earlier, the well in Samaria was an excellent setting for Christ to teach about the foundation of living water. Here, in chapter six, the multiplication of the loaves provides a way for Christ to present himself as the Bread of Life. This pattern parallels Jesus' point made in the last chapter when he emphasized that the Old Testament writers had foretold his coming. By readily using common places and events as examples of deeper truth, Jesus taught that the created order itself contains insight and lessons that point to him. "The God who revealed himself in the Old Testament also left his fingerprints all over His creation" (see Psalm 19:1–4, John 1:3–4, 9–10, Colossians 1:15–20, Hebrews 1:1–3 Tyndale 121).

This miracle was a significant turning point in the ministry of Jesus and is the only time in all four Gospels(Tyndale 121). After this miracle and teaching that flowed from it, many of those who had been following Jesus defected. It should also be said that some commentators see a connection between the Passover (mentioned in 6:4) and Jesus offering himself as the Bread of Life because the Passover symbolizes God's provision for life and salvation (see 1 Corinthians 5:7 Tyndale 121).

John 6:1–15

1.) Some time after this, Jesus crossed to the far shore of the sea of Galilee (that is, the Sea of Tiberias). 2.) And a great crowd of people followed him because they saw the signs He had performed by healing the sick. 3.) Then Jesus went up on a mountainside and sat down with His disciples. 4.) The Jewish Passover Festival was near. 5.) When Jesus looked up and saw a great crowd coming toward Him, He said to Philip, "Where shall we buy bread for these people to eat?" 6.) He asked this only to test him, for He already had in mind what He was going to do. 7.) Phillip answered Him, "It would take more than half a year's wages to buy enough bread for each one to have a bite!" 8.) Another of His disciples, Andrew, Simon Peter's brother, spoke up. 9.) "Here is a boy with five small barley loaves and two small fish, but how far will they go among so many?" 10.) Jesus said, "Have the people sit down." There was plenty of grass in the place, and they sat down (about five thousand men were there). 11.) Jesus then took the loaves, gave thanks, and distributed to those who were seated as much as they wanted. He did the same with the fish. 12.) When they all had enough to eat, He said to His disciples, "Gather the pieces that are left over. Let nothing be wasted. 13.) So, they gathered them and filled twelve baskets with the pieces of the five barley loaves left over by those who had eaten. 14.) After the people saw the sign Jesus performed, they began to say, "Surely this is the Prophet who is to come into the world." 15.) Jesus, knowing that they intended to come and make Him king by force, withdrew again to a mountain by Himself (Holman 1087-88)."

What is your Observation?

What is your Insight?

What is your Application?

Week 11:

1.   Where did Jesus cross the sea?

2.   Why did a great crowd follow Him?

3.   Where did Jesus sit down?

4.   What Festival was near?

5.   What did He say to Phillip?

6. How did Phillip answer?

7. What did the little boy have?

8. What did Jesus do with the little boy stuff?

9. How many ate?

10. What caused this to happen?

11. Was there any food left over? And what did Jesus tell them to do?

12. What did the people know? And what were they going to do with Jesus?

Life Application Bible Commentary on John: 6:26–70

Verses 26–29 states, "Very truly, I tell you, you are looking for me, not because you saw signs, but because you ate your fill of loaves (Tyndale 130)." The crowd, being satisfied once by what Jesus had done for them, wanted to see what else Jesus could do for them (maybe He'd provide more free meals?). But they did not realize what the miracle actually revealed to them. Even though they realized that perhaps Jesus was the Prophet (see 6:14), they were going to try to make Him king. Jesus refused to encourage them in their desire for the material satisfaction He could provide. His beginning response in effect was, "You were intent on the loaves themselves that you haven't yet seen who made them. The people may not have known it, but their needs went deeper. Jesus' signs were given to reveal that He could meet those deeper needs. On verses 30–31, amazingly, the crowd then asked Jesus "What miraculous sign then will you give that we may see it and believe you? What will you do? (Tyndale 131)." The crowd had just seen the miracle of the multiplication of the loaves, but they wanted more—not just one day's supply of bread, but a guarantee of continuous supply. Their argument was that their ancestors ate manna in the wilderness—which, of course, was available every day for nearly forty years (Tyndale 132). And they cited their Scriptures, quoting from such verses as Exodus 16:4 and Plasm 78:24–25, "He gave them bread from heaven to eat. A midresh (Jewish commentary) on Exodus 16:4 says that just as the former redeemer (Moses) caused manna to descend from heaven, so also the latter Redeemer will cause manna to descend. They expected this from Jesus if He was the Messiah.

John 6:25–59

25.) When they found Him on the other side of the lake, they asked Him, "Rabbi, when did you get here?" 26.) Jesus answered, "Very truly I tell you, you are looking for me, not because you saw the signs I performed but because you ate loaves and had your fill." 27.) "Do not work for food that spoils but for that endures to eternal life, which the Son of Man will give you. For on Him, God the Father has placed His seal of approval. 28.) Then they asked Him, "What must we do to do the works God requires?"

29.) Jesus answered, "The work of God is this: to believe in the one He has sent." 30.) So they asked Him, "What sign then will you give that we may see it and believe you? What will you do? 31.) Our ancestors ate the manna in the wilderness; as it is written: 'He gave them bread from heaven to eat.'" 32.) Jesus said to them, "Very truly I tell you, it is not Moses who has given you the bread from heaven, but it is my Father who gives you the bread from heaven. 33.) For bread of God is the bread that comes down from heaven and gives life to the world." 34.) "Sir," they said, "Always give us this bread." 35.) Then Jesus declared, "I am the bread of life, whoever comes to me will never go hungry, and whoever believes in Me will never be thirsty. 36.) But as I told you, you have seen Me and still you do not believe Me. 37.) All those the Father gives Me will never drive away. 38.) For I have come down from heaven not to do My will but to do the will of Him who sent Me. 39.) And this is the will of Him who sent Me, that I shall lose none of all those He has given Me, but raise them up on the last day. 40.) For my Father's will is that everyone who looks to the Son and believes in Him shall have eternal life, and I will raise them up at the last day." 41.) At this, the Jews there began to grumble about Him because He said, "I am the bread that came down from heaven." 42.) They said, "Is it not Jesus, the son of Joseph, whose father and mother we know? How can He now say, "I came down from heaven?" 43.) "Stop, grumbling among yourselves," Jesus answered, 44.) "No one can come to Me unless the Father who sent Me draws them, and I will raise them up on the last day." 45.) It is written in the Prophets: "They will all be taught by God. Everyone who has heard the Father, and learned from Him comes to Me. 46.) No one has seen the Father except the one who is sent from God. Only He has seen the Father. 47.) Very truly I tell you, the one who believes has eternal life. 48.) I am the bread of life. 49.) Your ancestors ate the manna in the wilderness, yet they died. 50.) But here is the bread that comes down from heaven, which anyone may eat and not die. 51.) I am the living bread that comes down from heaven. Whoever eats this bread will live forever. This bread is My flesh, which I will give for the life of the us, His flesh life of the world." 52.) Then the Jews began to argue sharply among themselves, "How can this man give us His flesh to eat?" 53.) Jesus said to them, "Very truly I tell you, unless you eat the flesh of the Son of Man and drink his blood, you have no life in you."

54.) "Whoever eats My flesh and drinks My blood has eternal life, and I will rise on the last day. 55.) For My flesh is real food and My blood is real drink. 56.) Whoever eats My flesh and drinks My blood remains in Me, and I in them. 57.) Just as the living Father sent Me and I will live because of the Father, so the one who feeds on Me will live because of Me. 58.) This is the bread that came down from heaven. Your ancestors ate manna and died, but whoever feeds on this bread will live forever." 59.) He said this while teaching in the synagogue in Capernaum.

Week 12:

1.   Why did they ask Jesus when He got here?

2.   How did Jesus know what they were looking for Him?

3. What was He telling them to do work for in verse 27?

4. Why did they ask Jesus what to do?

5. What is the work of God?

6. Why were they looking for signs?

7. Why did they say their ancestors ate manna in the wilderness?

8. What happened even though they ate manna?

9. Did they die? Why?

10. How did Jesus describe the bread from God?

11. What did they want Jesus to keep giving them?

12. Why did Jesus say whoever comes to Him never gets hungry?

Life Application Bible Commentary on John 6:60–61

Verse 60 states: When many of His disciples heard it, they said, "This teaching is difficult; who can accept it?" At this time in Jesus' ministry, He had several followers who could loosely be called *his disciples* (see 4:1). These "disciples" were not the twelve, and many of them would not receive His message. Verse 61 states: Jesus knowing that His listeners were struggling, asked, "Does this offend you?", or more literally, "Does this cause you to trip, cause you to stumble?". It is often used in the New Testament to indicate a falling away into unbelief. See for example Matthew 13:21, 24:10, Mark 6:3, Romans 14:20–21 (Tyndale 141).

Earlier, in answering questions that John the Baptist had asked through messengers, Jesus made this pointed remark, "And blessed is he who keeps from stumbling over me (Matthew 11:6 NASB)." Jesus was keenly aware that those not ready to respond fully to Him would stumble over Him or be offended by Him. Remember that it is possible to be offensive in the way we communicate the gospel, for which we would be at fault. But if we present Jesus lovingly and honestly, we must neither be shocked nor feel guilty if the Good News offends someone (Tyndale 141)."

John 6:60–70

60.) On hearing it, many of His disciples said, "This is a hard teaching. Who can accept it?" 61.) Aware that His disciples were grumbling about this, Jesus said to them, "Does this offend you? 62.) Then what if you see the Son of Man ascend to where He was before? 63.) The Spirit gives life, the flesh counts for nothing. The words I have spoken to you—they are full of the Spirit and life. 64.) Yet there are some of you who do not believe." For Jesus had known from the beginning which of them did not believe and who would betray Him. 65.) He went on to say, "This is why I told you that no one can come to Me unless the Father has enabled them." 66.) From this time many of His disciples, "turned back and no longer followed Him". 67.) "You do not want to leave either, do you?" Jesus asked the Twelve. 68). Simon Peter answered Him, "Lord, to whom shall we go? We have come to believe and to know that You are the Holy One of God." 70.) Then Jesus replied, "Have I not chosen you, the Twelve? Yet one of you is the devil." 71.) He meant Judas, the son of Simon Iscariot, who, though one of the Twelve, was later to betray Him (Holman 1089).

What are your Observations?

What are your Insights?

What are your Applications?

Week 13:

1.   Why did the disciples feel like this was a hard teaching?

2.   Why did Jesus feel that this offended the disciples?

3.   Why was the Son of Man ascending to where he was before important?

4.   Why is it important to know that the Spirit gives life?

5. Why did Jesus say that the flesh counts for nothing?

6. What was the word full of that He had spoken?

7. Why did Jesus say some did not believe?

8. Why did Jesus say some would betray Him?

9. Why did the disciples turn back?

10. Why did He ask the Twelve, "You do not want to leave too, do you?"

11. What did the Twelve come to believe?

12. Why did Jesus say, "Have I not chosen you, the Twelve?"

13. How did Jesus know that Judas was going to betray Him?

Life Application Bible Commentary on John 7:1–9

From this chapter forward, John shows Jesus as the suffering Messiah—suffering the unbelief of his own family, the divided opinions of the crowd, and the persecution of the Jewish religious leaders in Jerusalem (Tyndale 147). Because John clearly stated his purpose for writing this Gospel (20:30–31), even the rejection of Jesus proves that "Jesus is the Christ, the Son of God; and that by believing, you may have life in His name" (20:31 NLV, Tyndale 147). By portraying Jesus' rejection, John provided his first readers and us with a realistic picture of the costs of being a disciple (Tyndale 147).

Those who followed did so knowingly and willingly (Tyndale 147). John encourages us to believe, to stand firm, and to resist being like those who opposed and doubted Jesus while He lived on earth.

In this chapter and that which follows, John turns our attention to the Feast of Tabernacles (Tyndale 147). During this festival, the people commemorated God's provision (of water) for His people in the wilderness and presence among them (in the pillar of fire) by pouring out water on a rock and by lighting lamps. Jesus presents Himself as the spiritual reality of both God's provision (the water out of the rock) and God's presence (in the light).

John 7:1–44

1.) After this, Jesus went around in Galilee. He did not want to go about in Judea because the Jewish leaders there were looking for a way to kill Him. 2.) But when the Jewish Festival of Tabernacles was near, 3.) Jesus' brothers said to Him, "Leave Galilee and go to Judea, so that your disciples there may see the works You do. 4.) No one who wants to become a public figure act in secret. Since you are doing these things, show yourself to the world. For even his own brothers did not believe in him." 6.) Therefore, Jesus told them, "My time is not yet here; for you, anytime will do. 7.) The world cannot hate you, but it hates Me because I testify that its works are evil. 8.) You go to the festival, I am not going up to the festival, because My time has not yet fully come". 9.) After He had said this, He stayed in Galilee. 10.) However, after His brothers had left for the festival, He also went, not publicly, but in secret. 11.) Now at the festival, the Jewish leaders were watching for Jesus and asking, "Where is He?" 12.) Among the crowds, there was widespread whispering about Him. Some said, "He is a good man." Others replied, "no, He deceives the people." 13.) But no one said anything publicly about Him for fear of the leaders. 14.) Not until halfway through the festival did Jesus go up to the temple courts and begin to teach. 15.) The Jews there were amazed and asked, "How did this man get such learning without having been taught?" 16.). Jesus answered, "My teaching is not my own. It comes from the one who sent me. 17.) Anyone who chooses to do the teaching comes from God or whether I speak on my own. 18.) Whoever speaks on their own does so to gain personal glory, but he who seeks the glory of the one who sent him is a man of truth, there is nothing false about him. 19.) Has not Moses given you the law? Yet not one of you keeps the law. Why are you trying to kill me?" 20.) "You are demon-possessed," the crowd answered, "Who is trying to kill you?" 21.) Jesus said to them, "I did one miracle, and you are all amazed. 22.) Yet, because Moses gave you circumcision (though actually it did not come from Moses, but from the patriarchs), you circumcise a boy on the Sabbath. 23.) Now, if a boy can be circumcised on the Sabbath so that the law of Moses may not be broken, why are you angry with me for healing a man's whole body on the Sabbath? 24.) Stop judging by mere appearances, but instead judge correctly. 25.) At that point, some of the people of Jerusalem began to ask, "Isn't this the man they are trying to kill? 26.) Here he is, speaking publicly, and they are not saying a word to him. Have the authorities really concluded that he is the Messiah? 27.) But we know where this man is from, when the Messiah comes no one will know where He is from." 28.) Then Jesus, still teaching in the temple courts, cried out, "Yet, you know me, and you know where I am from. I am not here on my own authority, but he who sent me is true. You do not know Him, 29.) But I know Him, because I am from Him, and he sent me." 30.) At this, they tried to seize Him, but no one laid a hand on Him, because His hour had not come. 31.) Still, many in the crowd believed in Him. They said, "When the Messiah comes, will He perform more signs than this man?" 32.) The Pharisees heard the crowd whispering such things about Him. Then the chief priests and the Pharisees sent temple guards to arrest Him.

33.) Jesus said, "I am with you for only a short time, and then I am going to the one who sent me. 34.) You will look for me, but you will not find me, and where I'm at you cannot come." 35.) The Jews said to one another, "Where does this man intend to go that we cannot find Him? Will He go where our people live scattered, among the Greeks, and teach the Greeks? 36.) What did He mean when he said, 'You will look for me, but you will not find me, and where I am you cannot come?' 37.) On the last and greatest day of the festival, Jesus stood and said in a loud voice, "Let anyone that is thirsty come to me and drink. 38.) Believe in me as Scripture said, 'rivers of living water will flow from within them.' 39.) By this, He meant the Spirit, whom those who believed in Him were later to receive. Up to that time, the Spirit had not yet been given, since Jesus had not been glorified. 41.) Upon hearing His words, some of the people said, "Surely this man is the Prophet." 42) Others said He was the Messiah. Still others asked, "How can the Messiah come from Galilee? 43.) Does not the Scripture say that the Messiah will come from David's descendants and from Bethlehem, the town where David lived?"

44.) The people were divided because of Jesus. 44.) Some wanted to seize Him, but no one laid a hand on Him.

What are your Observations?

What are your Insights?

What are your Applications?

Questions:

1.   What area was Jesus around at this time?

2.   What festival was taking place?

3. Why did Jesus say His time was not yet here?

4. Why did Jesus go to the feast in secret?

5. Why was the crowd whispering about Jesus?

6. Why did Jesus say His teachings are not His own?

7. How did Jesus explain a man of truth?

8. Why did the crowd ask if Jesus was demon possessed?

9. What is the importance of a boy being circumcised on the Sabbath?

10. Why did the people ask if Jesus was the one that they were trying to kill?

11. Whose authority did Jesus say He was here by?

12. Why did they believe Jesus?

13. Why did Jesus say He is only with them a short time?

14. Why did the Jews try to understand where Jesus was going?

Life Application Bible Commentary on John 8:1–11

The earliest manuscripts of John's gospel do not include the story of the adulterous woman. It does not appear in any Greek church father's comment on the fifth century, and no Greek church father comments on the passage prior to the twelfth century. Even then, the comments state that the accurate manuscripts do not contain this story. When it was inserted in later manuscripts, the story of the adulterous woman appeared in different places: after John 7:52, after Luke 21:38, at the end of John; and when it does appear it is often marked off by asterisks to signal doubt about where it belongs. The story is part of an oral tradition that was circulated in Western church, eventually finding its way into the Latin Vulgate, and from there into later Greek manuscripts. The evidence against John having included this story in the gospel is conclusive. First, many scholars pointed out that the vocabulary used in this passage does not match the rest of John. Second, although the setting is plausible (other similar confrontations between Jewish leaders and Jesus occurred in Jerusalem), the insertion of the story at this point in John (after 7:52 and before 8:12) disrupts the narrative flow. Third, since the account does not appear in writing until later manuscripts, its "orphan" status is evidenced by it being in several locations.

Thus, this story was not originally part of this section of John. Consequently, it is not even included in the text of some Bible versions (For example, see the first edition of the RSV.). However, even though the passage was not written by John, it still may be regarded as a true story. It is unlikely that a later scribe would have made up such a story, given the strict views of the church regarding sexual immorality. The actions of the words of Jesus are consistent with what we know of him from the rest of the Gospels.

There is no new or unusual information in the passage that adds evidence against its inclusion. The encounter appears as an added snapshot of Jesus in John's collection, though we can tell that someone else probably took the picture. The event deserves at least consideration in teaching and preaching as an act that Jesus did at some point in His ministry, for it illustrates Jesus' compassion for sinful people (which includes us all) and His willingness to forgive any sinner; but the story should not be given the same authority as Scriptures.

John 8:1–11

Then they all went home. 1.) But Jesus went to the Mount of Olives. 2.) At dawn, he appeared again in the temple courts, where all the people gathered around him, and he sat down to teach them. 3.) The teacher of the law and Pharisees brought in a woman caught in adultery. They made her stand before the group. 4.) And said to Jesus, "Teacher, this woman was caught in adultery. 5.) In the Law of Moses, it commanded us to stone such women. Now what do you say?" 6.) They were asking this question as a trap. In order to have a basis for accusing him. But Jesus bent down and started to write on the ground with his finger. 7.) When they started questioning him again, he straightened up and said to them, "Let anyone without sin be the first to throw a stone at her." 9.) Again, he stooped down and started writing on the ground. 9.) At this, those that heard started to go away one at a time, the older one first, until only Jesus was left, with the woman still standing there. 10.) Jesus straightened up and asked her, "Woman , where are they? But no one condemned you?" 11.) "No one sir," she said. "Then neither do I condemn you." Jesus declared. "Go now and leave your life of sin."

What are your Observations?

What are your Insights?

What are your Application?s

Questions:

1.   Where did Jesus go?

2.   Where did He appear again?

3.   Why did the teachers of the law and Pharisees bring in this woman?

4.   What did the Law of Moses command them to do with the woman?

5.   How were they trying to trap Jesus?

6. What did Jesus do?

7. When Jesus stood up what did He say?

8. What did He do next?

9. Why did the crowd begin to go away?

10. How was it just Jesus and the women left there?

11. What did Jesus ask her?

12. How many condemned her?

13. Why did Jesus command her to leave her life of sin?

Life Application Bible Commentary John 8:12–59

"Jesus is the light of the world." (John 8:12–20)

This session ties in closely with the previous section (7:45–52)—minus the story of the woman caught in adultery, which John didn't write (170). In 7:45–52, Nicodemus had recommended that the religious leaders first hear Jesus before passing judgment on him. In this section, Jesus is heard, and he affirms the validity of his testimony based on his divine identity (171). In no other chapter of the Bible does Jesus make so many declarations about himself"(171). Here, he asserts his divine identity through a series of "I am" statements (all are from (NKJV, 171):

- "I am the light of the world." (8:12)
- "I am not alone." (8:16)
- "I am One who bears witness of Myself, and the Father who sent Me bears witness of Me." (818)
- "I am from above." (8:23)
- "I am not of the world." (8:23)
- "I am He [the Christ]." (8:24,28)
- "I am." (8:58)

John 8:12–30

12.) When Jesus spoke again to the people, He said, "I am the light of the world. Whoever follows me will never walk in darkness but will have the light of life." 13.) The Pharisees challenged Him, "Here you are, appearing as your own witness your testimony is not valid." 14.) Jesus answered, "Even if I testify on my own behalf, my testimony is valid, for I know where I came from and where I am going. 15.) You judge by human standards, I pass judgment on no one. 16.) But if I do judge, my decisions are true, because I am not alone, I stand with the Father, who sent me. 17.) In your own Law, it is written that the testimony of two witnesses is true. 18.) I am one who testifies for myself; my other witness is the Father, who sent me." 19.) Then they asked him, "Where is your father?" "You do not know me or my Father," Jesus replied. "If you knew me, you would know my Father also." 20.) He spoke these words while teaching in the temple courts near the place where the offerings were put. Yet no one seized him, because his hour had not yet come. 21.) Once more, Jesus said to them, "I am going away and you will look for me, and you will die in your sin. Where I go, you cannot come?" 22.) This made the Jews ask, "Will he kill himself? Is that why he says, "Where I go, you cannot come?" 23.) But He continued, "You are from below, I am from above. You are of this world; I am not of this world. 24.) I told you that you would die in your sins; if you do not believe that I am He, you will indeed die in your sins."

Questions:

1. What did Jesus say when He spoke again?

2. Why did Jesus promise, "Whoever walks in Him will never walk in darkness?"

3. How can Jesus give them the light of life?

4. How did the Pharisees challenge Jesus?

5. Why did they say Jesus' testimony was invalid?

6. How did Jesus testify on His own behalf?

7. Who did Jesus say He stands with?

8. Why was He not alone?

9. How is it written in man's Law that makes the testimony of two witnesses true?

10. Why did Jesus say you do not know me or my Father?

11. Where was Jesus teaching when He spoke these words?

12. Why was Jesus going away?

13. Why did the Jews ask, "Where He was going?"

14. Why did Jesus say they had to lift up the Son of Man to know who He was?

Life Application Bible Commentary on John 9:1–12, Jesus Heals The Man Born Blind

Thus far, Jesus has explained His identity in many ways to His listeners. Often, He would use a physical object, person, or setting to depict a certain spiritual aspect of His life and purpose. For example:

- While sitting by Jacob's well and talking to the Samaritan woman, Jesus explained that He could give her "living water" (4:10 NKJV, 191).
- After feeding over 5,000 people with two small loaves of bread, Jesus explained that hHe was "the bread of life" (6:35 NKJV, 191).
- At the Feast of Tabernacles, another symbolic act took place commemorating the time when Moses struck the rock in the wilderness and it brought forth water for the parched Israelites, Jesus told all the people, "If anyone thirsts, let him come to Me and drink" (7:37 NKJV, 191).
- Again, at the Feast of Tabernacles, another symbolic act took place commemorating the pillar of fire that guided the Israelites on their wilderness journey. Jesus told all the people, "I am the light of the world. He who follows Me shall not walk in darkness but have the light of life" (8:12 NKJV, 191).

All of Jesus' miracles also pointed to who He was. John follows Jesus' discourse about being "the light of the world" (8:12; 9:5) with the account of Jesus restoring sight to a man born blind. This story illustrates the spiritual truth of Christ being the Light of the World. As the blind beggar comes to "see" that Jesus is the Messiah, Jesus offers us spiritual sight to enable us to see Him as our Savior and Lord. We too are born spiritually blind and need the gift of sight that only the Light of the World can provide. The Light of the World becomes our light when we put our faith in Jesus Christ (LABC 191).

Religious leaders question the blind man, 9:13–34

Because the people discovered both a miracle and a mystery surrounding the healing of the blind man, they took him to what they considered the most dependable place for exploring such matters. The Pharisees quickly concluded that whatever else the healer might be, he certainly wasn't from God, for otherwise he would not work on the Sabbath. In their quest for "truth," these Pharisees tried a number of explanations to invalidate the miracle: (1) perhaps the blind man had not been blind from birth or had not been totally blind, (2) perhaps God did this miracle directly (but they would recognize no human agent (LABC 195).

When the formerly blind man pointed out the obvious answers that they had been so studiously avoiding, they responded by viciously berating him and expelling him from their presence' (LABC 196).

The astonishing fact of the man's newly given vision eluded this group as if they were blind. Later, Jesus pointed this out as their problem, over their strenuous objections (LABC 196).

Jesus teaches about spiritual blindness, 9:35–41

Unless we have suffered rejection for our faith, we may not be able to identify with the state of this blind man whom Jesus healed. In a single day, he went from being a disabled outcast to a celebrity who had miraculously received his sight, then to being a witness in court where he was treated like a criminal, and finally to being an outcast again (literally) for simply telling the truth as he clearly saw it (LABC 201).

At this point, Jesus intervened again. He found the man, faced him, and asked a question that would uncover whether this man was ready to receive complete vision. The man's understanding of the one who had healed him had already expanded considerably. Here was his chance to really see Jesus (LABC 202).

In the background of the man's willing trust and worship, we hear the Pharisees mumbling, incensed that Jesus was unwilling to recognize their spiritual stature. Instead, Jesus diagnosed their problem as ongoing profound blindness coupled with guilt (LABC 202).

John 9:1–41

1.) As He went along, He saw a man, blind from birth. 2.) His disciples asked him, "Rabbi, who sinned, this man or his parents, that he was born blind?" 3.) "Neither this man nor his parents sinned," said Jesus, "But this happened so that the works of God might be displayed in him. 4.) As long as it is a day, we must do the work of Him who sent me. Night is coming, when no one can work. 5.) While I am in the world, I am the light of the world." 6.) After saying that, He spit on the ground, and made some mud with the saliva, and put it on the man's eyes. 7.) "Go," he told him, "Wash in the Pool of Siloam" (this means "Sent"). So, the man went and washed and came home seeing. 8.) His neighbors and those who had formerly seen him begging asked, "Isn't this the same man who used to sit and beg?" 9.) Some claimed that he was. Others said, "No, he only looks like him." But he himself insisted, "I am the man." 10.) "How then were your eyes opened?" they asked. 11.) He replied, "The man they call Jesus made some mud and put it on my eyes. He told me to go to Siloam and wash. So, I went and washed, and then I could see." 12.) "Where is this man?" they asked him. "I don't know," he said. 13.) They brought to the Pharisees the man who had been blind. 14.) Now the day on which Jesus had made the mud and opened the man's eyes was a Sabbath. 15.) Therefore, the Pharisees also asked him how he had received his sight. "He put mud on my eyes," the man replied, "And I washed and now I see (Holman 1092–1093)." 16.) Some of the Pharisees said, "This man is not from God, for he does not keep the Sabbath." But others asked, "How can a sinner perform such signs?" So, they were divided." 17.) Then they turned again to the blind man, "What have you to say about him? It was your eyes he opened." The man replied, "He is a prophet." 18.) They still did not believe that he had been blind and had received his sight until they sent for the man's parents. 19.. Is this your son?" they asked, "Is this the one you say was born blind? How is it that now he can see?" 20.) "We know he is our son," the parents answered, "And we know he was born blind. 21.) But how he can see now, or who opened his eyes, we don't know. Ask him, he is of age, he will speak for himself." 22.) His parents said this because they were afraid of the Jewish leaders, who acknowledged that Jesus was the Messiah would be put out of the synagogue. 23.)

That was why his parents said, "He is of age; ask him" (Holman 1093). 24.) He replied, "Whether He is a sinner or not, I don't know. One thing I do know. I was blind but now I see!" 25.) Then they asked him, "What did he do to you? How did he open your eyes?" 26.) He answered, "I have told you already and you did not listen. Why do you want to hear it again? Do you want to become His disciples too?" 27.) Then they hurled insults at him and said, "You are this fellow's disciple! We are disciples of Moses! 28.) We know that God spoke to Moses, but as for this fellow, we don't even know where he comes from" (Holman 1093).

29.) The man answered, "Now that is remarkable! You don't know where he comes from, yet he opened my eyes. 30.) We know that God does not listen to sinners. He listens to the godly person who does His will. 31.) Nobody has ever heard of opening the eyes of a man born blind. 32.) If this man were not from God, he could do nothing."

33.) To this they replied, "You were steeped in sin at birth, how dare you lecture us!" And they threw him out. 34.) Jesus heard that they had thrown him out, and when He found him, He said, "Do you believe in the Son of Man?" 35.) "Who is he, sir?" the man asked. "Tell me so that I may believe in Him." 36.) Jesus said, "You have now seen him; in fact, He is the one speaking with you, 37.) Then the man said, "Lord, I believe," and he worshiped Him. 38.) Jesus said, "For judgment I have come into this world, so that the blind will see and those who see become blind (Holman 1093-94)."

39.) Some Pharisees who were blind, you would not be guilty of sin, but now that you claim you can see your guilt remains" (Holman 1094).

What Observations do you have about the chapter?

What Insights do you have about the chapter?

What Applications do you have about the chapter?

Questions:

1.   What did they see?

2.   Why did they ask the Rabbi who sinned?

3. How can the Rabbi say neither the man nor his parents?

4. How will God's work will be displayed?

5. What did he say we must do as long as it is light? Why?

6. What is coming?

7. Why is Jesus the light of the world?

8. Why did Jesus spit on the ground and make mud?

9. Why did Jesus tell the man to wash in the pool of Siloam?

10. What does Siloam stand for?

11. Why were the man's neighbors not able to recognize him?

12. Why did the man have to insist on who he was?

13. What was the man trying to tell about Jesus?

14. What were the Pharisees trying to prove?

15. Why did the Pharisees say that Jesus was not keeping the Sabbath day?

16. How could the Pharisees say that Jesus was not from God?

17. Why were they divided?

18. Why did the man say that Jesus was a prophet?

19. Why did they have to send for the man's parents?

20. Why did they ask the parents how their son was able to see now?

21. Why did the parents say that their son was of age and let him answer the question?

22. Why did the Pharisees say the second time give honor to God by telling the truth?

23. Why did the man say you do not hear?

24. Why did the Pharisees say they were disciples of Jesus?

25. Why did they say they were followers of Moses?

26. Why did they say God does not listen to sinners?

27. Why did they say this was never heard of before?

28. Why did the Pharisees say that the man was steeped in sin at birth?

29. Why did Jesus ask the man if he believed in the Son of Man?

30. Why did Jesus have to tell the man who He was?

31. Why did the man believe?

32. Why did Jesus say He came into the world so that the blind can see?

33. Why did the Pharisees ask if they were blind too?

34. Why did Jesus say their sin remains?

35. Why did Jesus say their sin remains?

Life Application Bible Commentary: John 10:1–42, Jesus is the Good Shepherd/10:1-21/(p. 151)

This chapter begins with an extended figure of speech or illustration (10:6), similar to a parable about shepherds and sheep. John provides two aspects of the illustration: the "gate" (10:3) and the "shepherd" (19:3-5), each with its own interpretation—the "gate" is interpreted in 10:7–10, and the "shepherd" in 10:11–18.

Paralleling leaders with shepherds and their people with sheep was a common analogy both in the Middle East and in the Bible (see for example 2 Samuel 5:2; 1 Kings 22:17; Zechariah 10:2). Shepherding was a common occupation. Many of the Old Testament leaders were shepherds, as were most of the ancestors of the entire nation of Israel (Genesis 46:32; 47:3). God is often called a shepherd or his people the sheep (Genesis 48:15, 49:24; Psalm 23:1, 80:1; Ecclesiastes 12:11; Isaiah 40:11, 53:6; Jeremiah 31:10; 1 Peter 2:25). Several of the elements in the illustration in verses 1–18 can be readily assigned a symbolic meaning:

- The "good shepherd" is Christ.
- The "sheep" are the Jewish believers.
- The "gate" is Jesus as the way to life.
- The "other sheep" are the Gentile believers.
- The "gatekeeper" is probably God.

The entire passage calls to mind the imagery of Ezekiel 34, where the prophet castigated the false shepherds (Israel's evil leaders) and predicted that the true Shepherd (the Messiah) would come and provide God's people (the sheep) with genuine care and leadership. In comparison to the Pharisees, who were bad leaders of God's people. The healed man who believed in Jesus (in the previous chapter) represented all believers who would come out of Judaism to follow Jesus, as sheep follow their shepherd (205).

Religious Leaders Surround Jesus at the Temple/ 10:22-42 (214)

As this section begins, there has been a temporary stalemate between Jesus and his opponents. They have become divided, so they are unable for a time to mount an effective attack against him. It must have been a period of intense frustration for the Jewish religious leaders. Finally, an opportunity for confrontation developed one day while Jesus was visiting the temple.

Answering to a direct question about his identity, Jesus briefly returned to the shepherd/sheep theme, but He concluded with a clear description of oneness between Himself and God. Once again, the stones used to execute blasphemers were about to be hurled, but Jesus faced down His accusers. When they tried to restrain Jesus, He left the temple and the area and traveled outside Jerusalem until the final week of His life. This strategic retreat cleared the way for Triumphal Entry.

John 10:1–42

"Very truly I tell you Pharisees, anyone who does not enter the sheep pen by the gate, but climbs in by some other way, is a thief and a robber.

2.) The one who enters by the gate is the shepherd of the sheep. 3.) The gatekeeper opens the gate for him, and the sheep listens to his voice. He calls his own sheep by name and leads them out. 4.) When he has brought out all his own, he goes on ahead of them, and his sheep follow him because they know his voice. 5.) But they will never follow a stranger; in fact, they will run away from him because they do not recognize a stranger's voice." 6.) Jesus used this figure of speech, but the Pharisees did not understand what He was telling them. 7.) Therefore, Jesus said again, "Very truly I tell you, I am the gate for the sheep. 8.) All who have come before Me are thieves and robbers, but the sheep have not listened to them. 9.) I am the gate, whoever enters through Me will be saved. They will come in and go out and find pasture. 10.) The thief comes only to steal and kill and destroy, I have come that they may have life, and live it to the full. 11.) I am a good shepherd. The good shepherd lays down his life for the sheep. 12.) The hired hand is not the shepherd and does not own the sheep. So, when he sees the wolf coming, he abandons the sheep and runs away. Then the wolf attacks the flocks and scatters it. 13.) The man runs away because he is a hired hand and cares nothing for the sheep. 14.) I am the good shepherd. I know my sheep and my sheep know me. 15.) Just as my Father knows me and I know the Father—I lay down my life for the sheep. 16.) I have other sheep that are not of this sheep pen. I must bring them also. They too will listen to My voice and there shall be one flock and one shepherd. 17.) The reason my Father loves Me is that I lay down my life—all of them only to take it up again. This command I received from my Father." 19.) The Jews who heard these words were again divided. 20.) Many of them said, "He is demon-possessed and raving mad. Why listen to him?" 21.) But others said, "There is not the saying of a man possessed by a demon. Can a demon open the eyes of the blind?" 22.) Then came the Festival of Dedication in Jerusalem. It was winter. 23.) And Jesus was in the temple courts walking in Solomon's Colonnade. 24.) The Jews who were there gathered around Him, saying, "How long will you keep us in suspense? If you are the Messiah, tell us plainly." 25.) Jesus answered, "I did tell you, but you do not believe. The works I do in my Father's name testify about me. 26.) But you do not believe it because you are not my sheep. 27.) My sheep listen to My voice, I know them, and they follow Me. 28.) I give them eternal life, and they shall never perish; no one will snatch them out of

My hand. 29.) My Father, who has given to me, is greater than all; no one can snatch them out of my Father's hand. 30.) I and the Father are one (Holman 1094)." 31.) Again, his Jewish opponents picked up stones to stone Him. 32.) But Jesus said to them, "I have shown you many good works from the Father. For which of these do you stone me?" 33.) "We are not stoning you for any good work," they replied, "but for blasphemy, because you, a mere man, claim to be God." 34.) Jesus answered them, "Is it not written in your law, I have said you are gods?" 35.) If he called them gods, to whom the word of God came... 36.) What about the one whom the Father set apart as His very own and sent into the world? Why then do you accuse Me of blasphemy because I said, "I am God's Son?" 37.) Do not believe me unless I do the work of my Father. 38.) But if I do them, even though you do not believe me, believe in the works that you may know and understand that the Father is in me, and I in the Father." 39.) Again, they tried to seize him, but he escaped their grasp. 40.) Then Jesus went back across the Jordan to the place where John had been baptizing in the early days. There He stayed. 41.) And many people came to Him. They said, "Though John never performed a sign, all that John said about this man was true. 42.) And in that place, many believed in Jesus.

What Observations did you see?

What Insights do you have?

What Applications can you use?

Questions on John 10:1–42:

1. Why did Jesus say to the Pharisees that the way to enter the sheep pen is by the gate?

2. Who is the shepherd of the sheep?

3. Who does the gatekeeper open the gate for?

4. Who listens to his voice?

5. Who does the shepherd bring out?

6. Why does the sheep follow him?

7. What will they do before following a stranger?

8. Why did the Pharisees not understand Jesus?

9. Why did Jesus have to tell the Pharisees that He was the gate for the sheep again?

10. What were the thieves and robbers trying to do?

11. Why did the sheep not listen to the thieves and robbers?

12. Did the sheep have to be saved?

13. What were the sheep going to find coming in and going out?

14. What do they thrive to do?

15. Who gives us life?

16. What does the good shepherd do for his sheep?

17. Who is not a shepherd?

18. Why does the hired hand abandon the sheep?

19. What does the wolf do?

20. What does the hired hand do when the wolf comes?

21. Who does Jesus know?

22. Who knows Jesus?

23. How do the sheep know Jesus?

24. What does Jesus do for His sheep?

25. Who also must Jesus bring?

26. Why do they listen to Jesus' voice?

27. Why does Jesus' Father love him?

28. Why were the Jews divided?

29. What did they start saying about Jesus?

30. What Festival was coming?

31. Why did the Jews want to know if He was the Messiah?

32. Why did Jesus tell them they do not believe?

33. What does Jesus give His sheep when they listen to His voice?

34. Who is the Father greater than?

35. In verse 30, what does Jesus say?

36. Why did the Jewish opponents want to stone Him again?

37. What did they call Jesus?

38. What were they saying Jesus claimed to be?

39. Who is the one the Father set apart?

40. Who did Jesus say He was?

41. How can they understand that the Father is in Jesus and Jesus is in the Father?

42. Why did they try to seize Jesus again?

43. What did Jesus do?

44. Who did those people believe in?

New Life Application Bible Commentary: Lazarus becomes ill and dies (John 11:1–16)

Up to this point in John's Gospel, Jesus has presented Himself as the giver of life to various people:

- To Nicodemus, He offered eternal life (3:16).
- To the Samaritan woman, the water of life (4:14).
- To the official's son and the lame man, the restoring of life (4:50; 5:5–8).
- To the hungry multitude, the bread of life (6:35).
- To the believers in Jerusalem, the rivers of living water (7:38).
- To the blind man, the light of life (8:12, 9:35–38).
- To the sheep who followed Him, the abundant life (10:10–11).

In chapter eleven, Jesus is *life* in its ultimate expression—He is "the resurrection and the life"—life after death. To the dead man, Lazarus, He offered resurrection of life. The Gospel tells us that Jesus raised others from the dead, including Jairus's daughter (Matthew 9:18–26; Mark 5:41–42; Luke 8:40–56) and a widow's son (Luke 7:11–17). These people represent a cross-section of ages and social backgrounds to whom Jesus gave back human life. All of them, including Lazarus, were raised but eventually died again. Lazarus' story stands out because John used it as a *sign* of Jesus' ultimate life-giving power and a picture of His own coming resurrection. And, as with all the miracles recorded in this gospel, it glorifies God. From John's perspective, this miracle was the turning point; it caused the Jewish leaders to take decisive action against Jesus. However, this chapter contains much more. We observe Jesus relating to different people under real stress.

Two sisters were frantic about their sick brother and then devastated by his death. The crowds continued to voice divided opinions about Jesus. The disciples sensed the possible outcome of Jesus' ongoing verbal skirmishes with the religious leaders.

Thomas displayed his courage and revealed his resolve when he said: "Let us also go, that we may die with him. (11:16 NIV)" The chapter teaches us that in the middle of very difficult circumstances, Jesus, the life-giver, desires to help and guide us. We must trust him. (Tyndale 223)."

Jesus comforts Mary and Martha/ 11:17–37

Although we get many glimpses of Jesus' compassion throughout the Gospels, His tender conversations with Mary and Martha are the most moving. His words reveal patient pastoral concerns. Elsewhere we see Him confront people with the truth; here, we see Him console as the gentle Master. Jesus did not ridicule or belittle grief. He affirmed our need for comfort by providing it to the sisters without hesitation. It is a tribute to the family that many from Jerusalem came to Bethany to pay their respects and offer their support to the sisters (Tyndale 235)."

Jesus raises Lazarus from the dead/ 11:38–44

As this chapter opens, we see Mary, Martha, and the crowd expressing conditional belief in the power of Jesus. They believed that Jesus could have worked a miracle if Lazarus had still been alive. But death intervened, and they thought it was irreversible. Little did they know that what they considered impossible would soon be overcome by God's power (Tyndale 235).

Religious leaders plot to kill Jesus/11:45–57

The seemingly ever-present religious leaders were not around to see Jesus' friend brought back to life. Perhaps they didn't think Jesus could do such a miracle. Some of the eyewitnesses, however, made it a point to report to the Pharisees in Jerusalem, only a couple of miles away. This fresh evidence of Jesus' power threw the Pharisees into a panic.

What follows is a priceless opportunity for us who know the full story to see how badly mistaken people can be in their assessment of events. We can also observe how desperately people will cling to a lie in the face of truth. The Pharisees and the Sanhedrin thought they were finally at the point of bringing matters to a conclusion with Jesus. But God fit their desperate plans into his own. They thought that killing Jesus would preserve their puny little sphere of power, but God knew that Jesus' death would provide salvation for the world (Tyndale 238).

John 11:1–5

1.) Now a man named Lazarus was sick. He was from Bethany, the village of Mary and her sister Martha. 2.) (This Mary whose brother Lazarus now lay sick, was the same one who poured on the Lord and wiped his feet with her hair.) 3.) So, the sisters said to Jesus, "Lord, the one you love is sick." 4.)..When He heard this, Jesus said, "This sickness will not end in death. No, it is for God's glory so that God's Son may be glorified through it." 5.) Now, Jesus loved Martha and her sister and Lazarus. 6.) So when He heard that Lazarus was sick, He stayed where He was two more days. 7.) And then He said to His disciples, "Let us go back to Judea." 8.) "But Rabbi," they said, "a short while ago the Jews there tried to stone You, and yet You are going back?" 9.) Jesus answered, "Are there not twelve hours of daylight? Anyone who walks in the daytime will not stumble, for they see this world's light. 10.) It is when a person walks at night that they stumble, for they have no light." 11.) After He had said this, He went on to tell them, "Our friend Lazarus has fallen asleep, but I am going there to wake him up." 12.) His disciples replied, "Lord, if he sleeps, he will get better." 13.) Jesus had been speaking of death, but His disciples thought He meant natural sleep. 14.) So, then He told them plainly, "Lazarus is dead. 15.) And for your sake, I am glad I was not there, so that you may believe. But let us go to him." 16.) Then, Thomas (also known as Didymus) said to the rest of the disciples, "Let us also go, that we may die with him." 17.) On His arrival, Jesus found that Lazarus had already been in the tomb for four days. 18.) Now Bethany was less than two miles from Jerusalem. 19.) And many Jews had come to Martha and Mary to comfort them in the loss of their brother. 20.) When Martha heard that Jesus was coming, she went out to meet Him, but Mary stayed at home. 21.) "Lord," Martha said to Jesus, "If you had been here, my brother would not have died. 22.) But I know that even now God will give you whatever you ask." 23.) Jesus said to her, "Your brother will rise again." 24.) Martha answered, "I know he will rise again in the resurrection on the last day." 25.) Jesus said to her, "I am the resurrection and the life. The one who believes in Me will live, even though they die; 26.) And whoever lives by believing in Me will never die. Do you believe this?" 27.) "Yes, Lord," she replied, "I believe that you are the Messiah, the Son of God, who is to come into the world." 28.) After she had said this, she went back and called her sister Mary aside. "The Teacher is here," she said, "And is this," she got up quickly and went to him. 30.) Now Jesus had not yet entered the village but was still at the place where Martha had met Him. 31.) When the Jews who had been with Mary in the house, comforting her, noticed how quickly she got up and went out, they followed her, supposing she was going to the tomb to mourn there. 32.) When Mary reached the place where Jesus was and saw Him, she fell at His feet and said, "Lord, if you had been here, my brother would not have died." 33.) When Jesus saw her weeping and the Jews who had come along with her also weeping, He was deeply moved in spirit and troubled. "Where have you laid him?" He asked. "Come and see, Lord," they replied. 35.) Jesus wept. 36). Then the Jews said, "See how He loved him!" 37.) But some of them said, "Could not He who opened the eyes of the blind man have kept this man from dying?" 38.) Jesus, once more deeply moved, came to the tomb. It was a cave with a stone laid across the entrance. 39.) "Take away the stone," He said.

"But, Lord," said Martha, the sister of the dead man, "By this time, there is a bad odor, for he has been there four days." 40.). Then Jesus said, "Did I not tell you that if you believe, you will see the glory of God?" 41.) So, they took away the stone. Then Jesus looked up and said, "Father, I thank you for listening to me. 42.) I knew that you always hear me, but I said this for the benefit of the people standing here, that they may believe that you sent me." 43.) When he had said this, Jesus called in a loud voice, "Lazarus, come out!" 44.) The dead man came out, his hands and feet wrapped with strips of linen, and a cloth around his face. Jesus said to them, "Take off the grave clothes and let him go." 45.) Therefore, many of the Jews who had come to visit Mary, and had seen what Jesus did, believed in Him. 46.) But some of them went to the Pharisees and told them what Jesus had done. 47.) Then the chief priests and the Pharisees called a meeting of the Sanhedrin. "What are we accomplishing?" they asked. "Here is this man performing many signs. 48.) If we let him go on like this, everyone will believe in him, and then the Romans will come and take away both our temple and our nation." 49.) Then one of them, named Caiaphas, who was high priest that year, spoke up, "You know nothing at all! 50.) You do not realize that it is better for you that one man dies for the people than that the whole nation perishes." 51.) He did not say this on his own; but as high priest that year, he prophesied that Jesus would die for the Jewish nation. 52.) And not only for that nation but also for the scattered children of God, to bring them together, and make them one. 53.) So, from that day on, they plotted to take his life. 54.) Therefore. Jesus no longer moved about publicly among the people of Judea. Instead, he withdrew to a region near the wilderness, to a village called Ephraim, where he stayed with his disciples. 55.) When it was almost time for the Jewish Passover, many went up from the country to Jerusalem for their ceremonial cleansing before the Passover. 56.) They kept looking for Jesus, and as they stood in the temple courts, they asked one another, "What do you think? Isn't He coming to the Pharisees who had given orders that anyone who found out where Jesus was should report it so that they might arrest him?"

Questions: John 11:1–57

1. What was the man's sick name?

2. Where was he from?

3. Who else was from there?

4. Who did Mary pour perfume on?

5. Who was her family?

6. Why did she send word to Jesus?

7. What did Jesus say when he heard?

8. Why did Jesus say it was for God's glory?

9. How will Jesus be glorified through death?

10. Why do you think Jesus stayed two more days after hearing about Lazarus?

11. Why do you think he told his disciples, "Let us go back to Judea?"

12. Why did the disciples warn him about almost being stoned by the Jews?

13. Why did Jesus use a parable in verse 9–10?

14. How was Jesus going to wake Lazarus?

15. Why did the disciples think Jesus was talking about normal sleep?

16. Why didn't Jesus know that Jesus was speaking of death?

17. Why did they say, "For their sake he was glad he was not there so that they might believe?"

18. Why did Thomas say, "Let us also go, that we may die with him?"

19. How long had Lazarus been in the tomb before Jesus arrived?

20. Why did many Jews go to Martha and Mary?

21. Why did Martha feel if Jesus had been there Lazarus would not have died?

22. Why did Martha say that God will give Jesus whatever he asks?

23. Why did Martha say that her brother will rise in the resurrection in the last days?

24. Why did Jesus say "I am the resurrection and the life?"

25. Why did Jesus say the one that believes in him will live?

26. Why, when Mary heard that Jesus was there, she went out to meet and fell at his feet?

27. Why did she also say, "Lord if you had been here, my brother would not have died?"

28. Why was Jesus deeply moved in the spirit and troubled after seeing Mary and the Jews weeping?

29. Why did Jesus weep?

30. Why did Martha say that by this time there was a bad odor, because he had been there four days?

31. Why did Jesus say, "Did I tell you that if you believe, you will see the glory of God?"

32. Why did Jesus pray the way he did?

33. What happened when Jesus called with a loud voice, "Lazarus come out?"

34. Why did the Jews plot to kill Jesus?

35. Why did many of the Jews believe Jesus afterwards?

Summary

We love our Lord and God, the *incarnation* that Jesus was born of the virgin Mary and grew up on earth just as we did and felt what we feel every day. He felt love and felt hate. He felt suffering and pain. He had a normal childhood with parents that raised Him and yet, fully God. When we hurt as individuals or as a nation, He understands because He knows all about suffering and feelings. When Jesus Christ was born, it happened in a manger around pagans that were looking for something miraculous to happen. Many people were waiting for a Savior to come into the world but of a different standard. They were looking for a rich and worldly king, absolutely not one living by a common citizen standard. Jesus had parents that were concerned about Him, and looked after Him. Jesus Christ put His relationship with God first above all others. Living here on earth, He went through trials and tribulation and did not sin. Jesus taught us what sin was and how to come to God. He taught us about God and how to have a relationship with God.

Whereas the miracles that were seen, Jesus did them in hopes that His disciple would believe. They struggled with His teachings, and some found them too hard to continue. Some left His teachings, but most stayed with Him and learned how to serve God. Jesus taught them how to heal the sick and raise the dead and cleanse the diseased. They were called *miracles.* At the wedding at Cana in Galilee, he turned water into wine rather than the master complimenting Him for bringing out the best wine for last. That was His first sign of showing His glory. The second sign is when He healed the official's son, and the official got news that His son will live. This was the second sign of God's glory. Jesus fed 5,000 people with five small barley loaves and two fish by blessing it and handing the food out and it did not stop coming until all the people were fed. This is the third sign that He showed God's glory that He was the living Christ whom God was well pleased with.

Furthermore, we read passages on Jesus Christ's *pre-existence* in John 1:1. Inthe beginning was the Word, which in Genesis 1:1, tells a story of God in the beginning. Philippians 2:5–11 talks about how Christ is the very nature of God, did not consider himself equal with God, something to be used to His advantage rather. He made Himself nothing by taking the very nature of a servant being made in human likeness.

All these Scriptures allow us to understand that Jesus Christ was in heaven before his Incarnation on earth because God had already had a plan on how He was going to save His children from their own sinful nature, through the blood of Jesus Christ. In the same manner, His ***preexistence*** allows us to know that He was more a human, but also, He was fully God.

Therefore, His ***resurrection*** was already part of God's plan in the making for our salvation. He was crucified, beaten to death, and on the third day, he ascended into heaven and sits at the right hand of the Father, interceding on our behalf. Those that trust in Jesus Christ's name shall not perish but have eternal life and forgiveness of sin. We have hope in the Father, Son, and Holy Spirit while we are here on earth. He has us to feed His sheep and Spiritual food that can maintain them until the day our Dear Jesus Christ comes for us to be with Him.

Therefore, as believers, Jesus Christ has called us to be ***disciples*** of His in the same manner that He called Peter, Andrew, Philip, and Nathanael to follow Him. They lived with Him and He taught them all about God and the Kingdom of Heaven. How He wants them to teach others about His living word by feeding His sheep. He wants them to spread the good news from one continent to the other. That is His legacy, mission, and goal. His incarnation, miracles, preexistence, resurrection, and discipleship all work hand in hand to bring new believers to the forefront to minister to others so they can share in His goodness and mercies every day.

Works Cited

Köstenberger, Andreas J. *Encountering John: The Gospel in Historical, Literary, and Theological Perspective.* Grand Rapids,, MI: Baker Academic, 2002.

Osborne, Grant R., and Bruce B. Barton. *John: Life Application Bible Commentary.* USA, 1993.

The NIV Rainbow Study Bible: Holy Bible, New International Version. China: Standard Pub, 2015.

Poem:

I love you Lord,
I love you Dear Jesus,
I worship you Lord,
I praise you because you wake me up each morning,
You give me breath to breathe,
And strength to walk,
You journey with me even when I do not realize it,
I always want a personal relationship with my God,
You pour out your companion on us,
You give us grace,
And show us mercy,
It is nothing that we deserve,
Your love endureth forever more,
I lift you up higher than heaven,
Because of your Love.

Poem: Deep Down

All I feel is dark hurt and pain inside,
This goes on every day, until you guided me to find my way, To you Dear Lord!
You sewed my heart back in place, because it was lost along the way. You gave me a stable place.
Now all I want is you in my life,
To lead me, guide me, and teach me your ways.
I can't get enough of your love.
Thanks for healing the pain inside,
I just want you deep down in my heart forevermore.
So I call on you every day,
To continue healing me and showing me the way.
Your blessings are here and may they endure forever!

Poem: I am on Shaky Grounds

I am on shaky grounds,
Trying to live my life the best way to please my God.
There is drama when I wake, it follows me through the day,
Even with each new friend I make,
I have to throw my hands up to you, And say, help me, Lord.
I can't live my life without so much confusion all around.
There seems to be no answer, I don't know what went wrong.
All I can do is throw my hands up to you,
And say, help me, Lord.
I try my best to live according to your great plan,
But nothing seems to go right,
And all I'm in is drama,
from someone that doesn't even know me.
All I can do is throw my hands up to you, And say, help me, Lord.
These sinful sick souls are reaching out to you, Saying, help me, Lord.
I don't know what went wrong,
but we need you to intervene!
All I can do is throw my hands up to you, And say, help me, Lord!

Poem: Lord You Called Me

Lord, you called me to read your word.
I came across a book that felt hurt, suffering, and pain.
I had to put it down and wait until I could come back for another round.
Lord, it's just too hard to bear all the ruins and shattered pictures, It just makes tears flow from my eyes; Lord, I can't stand the pain.
It is hard just to live day to day, I can't make it through this rat race,
Can you give me peace within, my soul is growing weary.
I need to just go on one more day. Please Lord, just take away the pain,
It hurts so much,
So much, Lord.
I need you to move by your Word so that you can make me a conqueror, over these feelings of hurt, pain, and suffering.

Come Lord, help me please!

Poem: Lord Every Day I Spend Time With You

Lord, every day I spend time reading all about you.
Your Words are so huge, and every breath I take I see you in a larger way.
I can't even begin to comprehend every letter and every Word you said.
At times, I feel so lost inside, I need you to help me find my way.
I need to know what you are revealing to me.
It is so big that I want you to just pour and pour your wisdom on me.
Give me wisdom, knowledge, and understanding of your vision, mission, and purpose.
Of your vision,
Of your vision Lord,
I need you to give me sight, so I can help others with your flight,
So I can help others find their way to you Lord!

Poem: Have You Heard of the Ten Commandments

I have heard of the Ten Commandments.
I have heard through your Words, but as you begin to understand how awesome and wonderful the Word of God is,
You have to take a deeper breath to go on!

John 6:68–69

68.) "Simon Peter answered him, "Lord, to whom shall we go? You have the Word of eternal life! 69.) "We have come to believe and to know that you are the Holy One of God."

You Lord are the only way to eternal life.

There is no other way but through the Father, Son, and Holy Spirit!

Please lead the way because we can't find the way without You!

Final Research Paper: Romans 8:31–39

Moo begins by talking about the beautiful and familiar celebration of the believer's security in Christ, which comes in response to Paul's rehearsal of the blessings that have been granted to the believer through the gospel. Since Paul has been enumerating these blessings from virtually the first verses of the climax of the letter up to this point.

Romans 8:31–39

31. What then shall we say in view of these things? If God is for us, who is against us?

32. He who did not even spare his own son, but handed him over for all of us—how will he not also freely give us all things with him?

33. Who will bring any charge against God's elect?

34. Who is the one condemning? Christ Jesus is the one who died and more, was raised, who is at the right hand of God, who also is interceding for us.

35. Who will separate us from the love of Christ? Will tribulation, distress, persecution, famine, nakedness, perils, or the sword?

36. Even as it is written, "For your sake, we are being put to death all day long: we are considered as sheep for slaughter."

37. But in all these things we are more than conquerors through the one who loved us.

38. For I am persuaded that neither death, life, nor powers,

39. Nor height, life, depth, nor any created things will be able to separate us from the love of God, in Christ Jesus our Lord.

Verse 31 refers only to these blessings enumerated in the immediately preceding verses (28 or 29–30). Moo (538) suggests turning the Bible reading in accordance with 8:31.

Romans 5 tells that through faith in Christ, Christians have been assured, justified, and declared righteous by God once and for all. They no longer need to live in fear of God's wrath and judgment. Rather, they enjoy peace with God (Moo 538, Holman 1499). Not only is the believer guaranteed ultimate vindication: 'He or she is also promised victory over all the forces of the world (Moo 538). And the basis for this man-faceted assurance is the love of God for us in Christ, God's or Christ's, love is the motif of this paragraph, mentioned three times (vv. 35, 37, 39; cf. Rom 5:5-8; Moo 539).

All this Paul sums up in the simple statement, "If God be for us (Moo 539)." The preposition I translated "on behalf of " (Moo 539), Paul uses it frequently to depict the vicarious work of Christ (especially 5:6–8).

Here, it suggests that God is "on our side," that he is working "for" us. "If this be so," Paul asks, "Who is against us?" Obviously, Paul does not mean that nobody will, in fact, oppose us. As Paul knows from his own experience (to which he alludes in v. 35), opposition to believers is both varied and intense. What Paul is suggesting by this rhetorical question is that 'nobody—and nothing—can ultimately harm, or stand in the way of the one whom God is "for." This is how Chrysostom put it.

The church, like Judaism, was interested in the story of Isaac because it was an example of Abraham's steadfast obedience to God that could also be understood as a story of martyrdom—the death of innocence to fulfill the will of God (Wright 170). "My interest in the exegesis of the Akedah will not be solely literary, nor will it be exhaustive, for there has already been a good deal of criticism on the topic. Rather, I went to recover what the pre-Christian Jewish tradition had to say about the question of Martyrdom, how that theme related to the story of Abraham's sacrifice of Isaac and, in turn, how the question of the martyrdom of Isaac, affected Paul's version of Christianity. Of course, to the completely uninitiated, the story is of dubious importance to Christianity. But those who know a little Jewish tradition will know that occasionally Isaac was viewed by the rabbis as being sacrificed and his ashes used to atone for Israel's sins (Wright 169- 70)."

Wright goes on to interpret Paul, by talking about how Judaism has made explicit their theme, rather 'Biblical version or the Maccabean martyrs of the crusades (Wright 170)."

The three they named are a model of the suffering messiah, a model of a Jewish martyr of the crusades, and the medieval European pogroms (Wright 170). The medieval Europeans envision themselves as Isaac. He was prepared to be slaughtered by a nick of a knife for sacrifice Kierkegaard saw it as a "leap of faith" but Vermes looked at it differently such as "paying little attention to chronological," or "to follow the development of exegetical principles by means of historical criticism (Wright 171)." This is how he identifies the particular text read by a particular audience and to fill in the historical, social, cultural, and religious—or the entire semantic context of the time.

Wright goes on to interpret Paul, by talking about, how different is the Christian material (Wright 177). Here, one finds that the identification of the martyred figure of the Messiah is typology. Paul's use of the scripture immediately shows this tradition to systematic comparison. At most one can say that he is using the Isaac story with considerable exegetical functionalism. Possible references to Isaac come up only twice, and only in indirect ways in Paul. "He who did not spare his son but gave him up for us all (Wright 178)." Clearly sounds the note of vicarious atonement, but it neither mentions Isaiah 53 nor the temple service, nor blood (Wright 178). Paul appears to draw a kind of implicit analogy between God's action and the action of Abraham; God recompensed mankind in a kind of "measure for measure" (middah k'neged middah) argument that Christ died for sins does not really need proof for Paul. It can be found in 1 Cor 15:3b and frequently elsewhere. But only here in 1 Corinthians does he say that saving description he has in mind, although this is possible. Almost all scholars agree that he is using traditions, which were taught to him by the community which he joined and which, therefore, antedate his entrance into Christianity.

Wright noted that in Romans 8:32, in discussing the sacrifice of Isaac, the focus of the passage is Abraham, not Isaac, just as in earlier Jewish interpretation. The "us in Romans is left unspecified." But, by means of Galatians 3:13–14, the reference can be further clarified that "the blessing of Abraham might come upon the Gentiles," is a paraphrase of Gen. 22:18, and in your offspring shall all the nations of the earth be blessed. The expressed "blessing of Abraham" may have been taken from Gen 23:4, but "in Christ Jesus" has been substituted for the original "in your offspring (Deut. 21:23) curses a man hanged on the tree." But Paul, who applies the reference to Jesus, says that the curse has been turned into a blessing, perhaps there by playing upon the Genesis story of the Lamb caught in the thicket. In this case, however, the analogy would be between the ram and Jesus, since both are seen as the sacrifice provided by God.

The novel aspect for Paul is an obvious aspect of the story of a crucified Messiah, the obvious aspect of the story missing from the pre-Christian Jewish exegesis, where Isaac is never understood as a type of the Messiah.

It is very clear that Paul takes the crucified Jesus to be Messiah and Son of God because of his faith commitment, not because of a pre- existing development of the midrash. Only because of his prior faith can he say that as Abraham had offered up his son, so too God offered up His Son for Isaac's children so that all families of man would be blessed. It is a new idea totally absent from Jewish exegesis, even when Jewish exegesis stresses the vicariousness of the sacrifice.

It seems as if Vermes describes a figure of Isaac the vicarious martyr which can merely be taken over into Christianity (Wright 179). Since this is clearly not the impression that the evidence gives, the criticism of Davies and Chilton has some validity. They note that the missing terms in the pre-Christian interpretation are just as important as the attested ones because they underline the thought processes of the Jewish interpreters before Jesus and emphasize the central aspect of the new Christian interpretation. He goes on to say he cannot find any to interpret Isaac's passage messianically and none sums up past experience like Vermes does.

Nowhere else is there to appear a figure like the "suffering servant" and there is no figure in Judaism called The Suffering Servant. God's enduring love and faithfulness is a fitting conclusion to Romans 5–8 (Moo 141). In these chapters, Paul brings home what the believer's assurance should look like in Jesus Christ. They should have absolute assurance of the truth for the future. God has transferred us from the realm of Adam, sin, and death into the realm of Christ, righteousness, and life. Although the old realm has not been eradicated and still has the power to attract us away from the path to righteousness and life, nothing can stand in the way of our ultimate salvation. We have a "hope of glory" (5:2) that we can withstand any challenge. Most of us associate the language of 8:31–39 with funerals. While the reminder that nothing can separate us from God's love for us in Christ is certainly appropriate when we are dealing with the death of a loved one or friend, this same reminder is equally important at every juncture of life. While facing the doubts, uncertainties, and difficulties of a world hostile to God and his values, we constantly need the reassurance that "God is for us."

Verse 32 is a kind of conditional sentence with "God handing over his Son" being the "if" clause and "how will He not also freely give us all things" the "then" clause (Moo 540). But by introducing the second with "how," Paul suggests how inconceivable it would be for this "Then" clause to remain unfulfilled. "If God has, indeed, given His Son for us, how can anyone doubt that He will not also freely give us all things along with Him? (Moo 541)" How broad is the scope of the "all things" that God so graciously bestowed on us ?" Paul could be alluding to our share in Christ's sovereignty over creation. But it is not clear that these ideas play a role in our present passage. Certainly, Paul's focus is on those things necessary for our salvation, but, as with "the good" in verse 28, we should not restrict the meaning to salvation as such but include all those blessings—spiritual and material—that we require on the path toward that final salvation. Why be dubious about the chattels, when you have the Lord (Moo 541)?"

Victory over trials and tribulations

29.) "To stand on that day is to be found justified by God's grace and so qualified for final salvation (Volf 52)." 30.) This is already in verse 2 Paul alludes to the significance of divine grace for final salvation: Christians "stand in grace" clear up to their vindication in the final judgment (Volf 53). According to Paul, grace will never cease to govern God's dealings with believers. 31.) And for this very reason Christian hope will not disappoint, "well es eben Gottes Gnade ist, auf die der Christ hofft."

32.) In verse 5:9–10, Paul draws out the significance of God's gracious love as the guarantee that Christian hope will not disappoint. Having now been justified by his blood, how much more shall we be saved through him from the wrath; for if, while we were enemies, we were reconciled, shall we be saved by his life. With the help of these two arguments *maiori ad minus,* he shows that God's accomplishment of the scarcely imaginable feat of demonstrating love toward rebellious sinners in the cross. Christ guarantees the future salvation of those who are God's own people in fulfillment of their hope. 33.) For those who will benefit from completion of the work of salvation centered in the cross are no longer "sinners" but "justified," not "enemies" but "reconciled." 34.) Moreover, the consummation of salvation is not through the Son's death but His life (v.10, Volf 53). 35.) Since God's saving love is already seen to exceed all expectations, back to the cross, Christians see a reason to look forward with confidence to the realization of the hope of salvation.

36.) Because Christian hope will not be put to shame, Paul can make it the object

of boasting (5:2, Volf 53). 37.) Only a hope which is certain can be a hope in which we boast. 38.) And only hope in God can fulfill this criterion. "Christian" boast can therefore rightly be said to be in God, who fulfills hope (v. 11cf. Phil 3:3; Gal 6:14; Cor 1:31; 2 Cor 10:17). Paul discredits all other objects of boasting (4:2, 3; 1 Cor. 1:29; 3:21; Phil 3:3), which amount to self-glorifying, in particular, Jewish boasting in the law and in (special privilege before) God (cf. 2:23, 17, Volf 54). By contrast, Christians boast appropriately in God and God's saving deeds (Volf 54).

In Romans 8:28, 35–38-,Paul announced the theme of present suffering as characteristic of Christian experience in Roman 5:1–11 (Volf 56). In verses 35–39, he develops it in relation to the question of continuity and tension in salvation (Volf 56). The sorrows mentioned at 5:3 are now named individually: tribulation, hardship, persecution, famine, nakedness, danger, the sword (8:35, Volf 56). Paul can describe his own life as a Christian and apostle of Christ similarly (cf. 2 Cor. 4:7–12; 6:4–10; 11:23–33). Paul has in mind the suffering of believers is clear from the quotation of Ps. 43:23 LXX at 8:36 (Volf 56). The Psalm speaks of the suffering of faithful martyrs: For your sake, we are put to death the whole day, we are reckoned as sheep for slaughter (Volf 56).

Conclusion

What Paul is saying is that we are guaranteed by God that we have salvation for those who believe in the name of our Lord Jesus Christ, so we can be assured that we are justified by our faith in Christ Jesus. And nothing will separate us.

Why? He was writing about how a sinful person can get into a right relationship with God to be forgiven for our sins. It is nothing we do but it is God that calls us and justifies us by faith in him that we shall be saved. God gives us the free gift of salvation. He is the one who chose us and calls us. It is nothing that we do because we are saved by the grace of God. He does not have to do it, but He chose to do it of His own accord.

How? He does it is through His election, He knows what He and who he is going to choose. The Bible says we are called from the foundation of the world. It is a process that we go through until the day we die. He loves us and wants us to be saved and he does it through His effective calling. Romans teach us that nothing will separate us from His love.

So what? Now this allows me to know that God has chosen me, and I was chosen from the foundation of the world to be saved. He has taught me how to be a teacher of His word and to give to others my Christian beliefs so that they may know who God is and come to have a personal relationship with Him. One thing I know is to take it wherever I go. This is a way of life and my belief. I can come alongside others and journey with them through their struggles and talk to them about what I know and hope of them coming to saving faith in Jesus Christ! Amen.

Works Cited

Gundry, Volf Judith M. *Paul and Perseverance: Staying in and Falling Away.* Louisville, KY: Westminster/John Knox Press, 1990.

Beare, Francis Wright. *From Jesus to Paul: Studies in Honour of Francis Wright Beare.* Edited by John Coolidge Hurd and Peter Richardson. Wilfrid Laurier University Press, 1984.

Moo, Douglas J. *Encountering the Book of Romans: A Theological Survey.* Grand Rapids, MI: Baker Academic, 2007.

Moo, Douglas J. *The Epistle to the Romans.* Grand Rapids, MI: W.B. Eerdmans Pub. Co., 1996.

Poem: Alfa

Dear Lord, God,
You are the petals of a blooming flower,
You are the shining glaze in the sky,
Your hands hold the solar system together,
Your breath speaks creation to the galaxy!
Just one puff of Your power begins the stars to rotate on its axis! Awesome is Your majestic voice!
You are The Alpha and Omega!
You are who you say you are! The first and the last! And there is none like you! You are The Great I Am! The beginning and the Ending,
The Great I Am!

www.ingramcontent.com/pod-product-compliance
Lightning Source LLC
LaVergne TN
LVHW091600060526
838200LV00036B/925